Welcome to
LIFESEARCH!

If you urgently need to prepare to lead a LIFESEARCH group, turn the page and read QUICKLEAD®. QUICKLEAD® will give you enough information to get started.

LIFESEARCH hopes to help you and other persons within a small group explore topics about which you are concerned in your everyday living. We've tried to make LIFESEARCH

✓ immediately helpful to you;

✓ filled with practical ideas;

✓ Christian-oriented and biblically based;

✓ group building, so you will find companions in your mutual struggles and learning;

✓ easy for anyone to lead.

You have probably chosen to join with others in studying this LIFESEARCH book because you feel some need. You may feel that need in your life strongly. Our hope for you is that by the time you complete the six chapters in this book with your LIFESEARCH group, you will have

✓ a better handle on how to meet the need you feel;

✓ some greater insights into yourself;

✓ a deeper understanding of how Christian faith can help you meet that need;

✓ a more profound relationship with God;

✓ new and/or richer relationships with the other persons in your LIFESEARCH group.

If you discover nothing else as part of this LIFESEARCH experience, we want you to learn this fact: *that you are not alone as you face life.* Other people have faced and still face the same problems, struggles, demands, and needs that you face. Some have advice to offer. Some have learned things the hard way—things they can now tell you about. Some can help you think through and talk through old concerns and new insights. Some can listen as you share what you've tried and what you want to achieve. Some even need what you can offer.

And you will never be alone because God stands with you.

The secret to LIFESEARCH is in the workings of your group. No two LIFESEARCH groups will ever be alike. Your LIFESEARCH group is made up of unique individuals—including you. All of you have much to offer one another. This LIFE-SEARCH book simply provides a framework for you and your group to work together in learning about an area of mutual concern.

IF YOU ARE LEADING A LIFE-SEARCH GROUP, please read the articles in the back of this book.

These LIFESEARCH group leadership articles may answer the questions you have about leading your group.

IF YOU ARE PARTICIPATING IN A LIFESEARCH GROUP, BUT NOT LEADING IT, please read at least the article "If You're Not Leading the Group." In any case, **you will benefit most if you come to your group meeting having read the chapter ahead of time and having attempted any assignments given in the previous chapter's "Before Next Time" sections.**

We want to remain helpful to you throughout your LIFESEARCH group experience. If you have any questions about using this LIFESEARCH book, please feel free to call Curric-U-Phone at 1-800-251-8591 and ask for the LIFESEARCH editor.

QUICKLEAD®

Look here for **QUICK** information about how to **LEAD** a session of LIFE-SEARCH. On LIFESEARCH pages, look for the following:

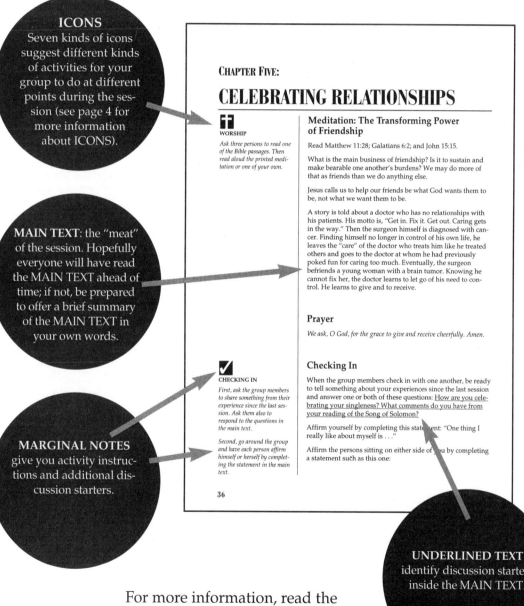

ICONS
Seven kinds of icons suggest different kinds of activities for your group to do at different points during the session (see page 4 for more information about ICONS).

MAIN TEXT: the "meat" of the session. Hopefully everyone will have read the MAIN TEXT ahead of time; if not, be prepared to offer a brief summary of the MAIN TEXT in your own words.

MARGINAL NOTES give you activity instructions and additional discussion starters.

UNDERLINED TEXT identify discussion starters inside the MAIN TEXT.

CHAPTER FIVE:

CELEBRATING RELATIONSHIPS

WORSHIP

Ask three persons to read one of the Bible passages. Then read aloud the printed meditation or one of your own.

Meditation: The Transforming Power of Friendship

Read Matthew 11:28; Galatians 6:2; and John 15:15.

What is the main business of friendship? Is it to sustain and make bearable one another's burdens? We may do more of that as friends than we do anything else.

Jesus calls us to help our friends be what God wants them to be, not what we want them to be.

A story is told about a doctor who has no relationships with his patients. His motto is, "Get in. Fix it. Get out. Caring gets in the way." Then the surgeon himself is diagnosed with cancer. Finding himself no longer in control of his own life, he leaves the "care" of the doctor who treats him like he treated others and goes to the doctor at whom he had previously poked fun for caring too much. Eventually, the surgeon befriends a young woman with a brain tumor. Knowing he cannot fix her, the doctor learns to let go of his need to control. He learns to give and to receive.

Prayer

We ask, O God, for the grace to give and receive cheerfully. Amen.

CHECKING IN

First, ask the group members to share something from their experience since the last session. Ask them also to respond to the questions in the main text.

Second, go around the group and have each person affirm himself or herself by completing the statement in the main text.

Checking In

When the group members check in with one another, be ready to tell something about your experiences since the last session and answer one or both of these questions: How are you celebrating your singleness? What comments do you have from your reading of the Song of Solomon?

Affirm yourself by completing this statement: "One thing I really like about myself is . . ."

Affirm the persons sitting on either side of you by completing a statement such as this one:

36

For more information, read the **LEADERSHIP ARTICLES** in the back of this LIFESEARCH BOOK.

ICONS

ICONS are picture/symbols that show you at a glance what you should do with different parts of the main text at different times in the LIFESEARCH sessions.

The seven kinds of icons are

 WORSHIP—A prayer, hymn, or other act of worship is suggested at this place in the MAIN TEXT.

 CHECKING IN—At the beginning of each session, LIFESEARCH group members will be asked to "check in" with one another about what is happening in their lives. Sometimes group members will also be asked to "check in" about how their LIFESEARCH group experience seems to them.

 DISCUSSION POINT—Either the MAIN TEXT or a MARGINAL NOTE will suggest discussion starters. You will probably find more DISCUSSION POINTS than you can use in the usual LIFESEARCH session.

 GROUP INTERACTION—Either the MAIN TEXT or a MARGINAL NOTE will suggest a group activity that goes beyond a simple discussion within the whole group.

 BIBLE STUDY—At least once each session, your LIFESEARCH group will study a Bible passage together. Usually, DISCUSSION POINTS and/or GROUP INTERACTIONS are part of the BIBLE STUDY.

 WRITTEN REFLECTION—The MAIN TEXT will contain one or more suggestions for individuals to reflect personally on an issue. Space will be provided within the MAIN TEXT for writing reflections. Sometimes individuals will be invited to share their written reflections if they wish.

 BEFORE NEXT TIME—In most sessions, your LIFESEARCH group members will be asked to do something on their own before the next time you meet together.

INTRODUCTION

As a child, I spent enough hours sitting in the corner in "time out" to know I did not like the word *discipline*. This word has a negative connotation for many of us; we think of punishment bestowed at the hands of others. The truth is, however, we all need discipline if we are to grow. Children need the discipline of a loving parent to grow into productive and well-adjusted adults. Adults need discipline to learn new skills and to acquire knowledge.

Artists, musicians, and athletes who want to develop their skills need discipline to do so. Their talents remain undeveloped without discipline; so it is with our faith. As a people of faith, we must cultivate the skills and practices of our spiritual life in order to grow. These practices, often called spiritual disciplines, include, but are not limited to, prayer and meditation, worship, discernment, and Bible study. Through these practices we develop our relationship with God and our spiritual nature. Although the practices require discipline, they are not a penance for wrongs we have committed. Nothing could be further from the truth. The spiritual disciplines are intended to lead us to a more joyful and abundant life.

When practiced regularly, spiritual disciplines can guide us into deeper intimacy with the Source of all love. But they must be implemented in order to work. Much like an athlete needs regular exercise to stay fit, we must exercise our spiritual disciplines regularly in order to be fit. Like the developing artist who draws the tree many times before it becomes a painting stirring the hearts of others by its beauty, we must practice the disciplines until our heart is transformed by God.

Unfortunately, discipline does not come easily to many of us. Yet, if we want to mature in our faith, I can think of no better way than to undertake the practice of a spiritual discipline. Though we may have been converted to Christianity in a moment, it takes a lifetime to become a mature Christian. Even if we have grown up in the faith, it takes many years for our life to be transformed and shaped into the likeness of Christ, the goal of the Christian life. Commitment, work, and discipline are needed to reach this goal. With the use of the spiritual disciplines, our life can be transformed.

A word of caution is offered here, lest we think we can acquire this transformation by our own efforts. We cannot. The spiritual disciplines in and of themselves, even when practiced strictly, do not transform us into mature Christians. They simply open the door so that God can do the transforming. It is always God who transforms. By God's grace we are made whole and not by our efforts alone. Spiritual disciplines are a means of receiving God's grace. They allow us to stay open to the mysterious and transforming work of love in our life, and they help us respond to that love.

The Bible is full of references to the spiritual disciplines, including fasting, worship, and prayer; but it offers almost no instructions on how to participate in those practices. While it is clear spiritual disciplines are part of the faithful life, we are not given the instruction book with the practical how-to's. This study will include many such practical directions for your instruction and practice.

A word of caution is in order, however. Although the mechanics of the spiritual disciplines are important, they are not as important as the attitude of the heart. The disciplines are meant to bring us into abundant life; however if they are turned into law, they can kill the soul. I hope you will keep this fact in mind as we explore a new discipline each session. Pay close attention to your attitude as you engage in each new discipline.

Perhaps you have been wondering if the spiritual disciplines are meant for you. Let me assure you, spiritual disciplines are intended for ordinary people, not just theological giants. They are for human beings who live regular lives, hold down jobs, clean house, bathe the dog, and cook dinner. All that is required to enter into the spiritual disciplines is a yearning for God.

Augustine of Hippo, a bishop in the early Christian church, prayed to God: "You have made us for yourself, and our hearts are restless till they rest in you." In this study, the six spiritual disciplines we explore will help us address our yearning for God. The three inward disciplines we examine (spiritual reading, prayer and meditation, and fasting) will enable us to find a more intimate relationship with God—which is the only thing that ultimately satisfies our deepest longings. The three outward disciplines we examine (hospitality, spiritual guidance, and worship) will help us look at our life with God in relationship to others. Though this list of spiritual disciplines is not exhaustive, I hope you will enjoy this introduction to the spiritual life.

—Karla Kincannon

Karla M. Kincannon is an artist and an ordained United Methodist minister. A clergy member of the Virginia Annual Conference since 1980, Karla has pastored churches and has served in campus ministries at both state and private colleges. She holds a Bachelor of Arts degree in Art from Virginia Wesleyan College and a Master of Divinity degree from Garrett-Evangelical Theological Seminary.

Karla currently lives in Nashville, Tennessee, with her spouse, Jim Noseworthy, her stepson, and her two golden retrievers. She is the executive director of The Center for Arts and Spiritual Awareness, an organization that helps individuals and churches incorporate the visual arts into the life of faith.

CHAPTER ONE

SPIRITUAL READING: READING FOR TRANSFORMATION NOT INFORMATION

WORSHIP

When the group is ready to begin, open the session with this Scripture reading and prayer. You can read the Scripture, or ask someone else to read it. You may use a prayer of your own if you choose.

CHECKING IN

If you have a large piece of paper or a chalkboard available, list the spiritual disciplines mentioned and any definitions offered. When everyone has shared, have the entire group work together to develop a definition for spiritual discipline. At the end of the six sessions, check to see how the group's definition of spiritual discipline has changed.

Read Philippians 4:8-9.

Living God, direct our minds toward thoughts of you and your magnificent creation. Help us hold in our hearts pure and pleasing things so that we may grow daily in the likeness of Christ. We give you thanks and praise. Amen.

Checking In

For this first session, be prepared to share in turn (1) your name and (2) brief information about your family, work, and leisure activities. Also, try to answer the question, What is a spiritual discipline? You may offer a definition or name a spiritual discipline you have heard about, practiced, or would like to know more about.

DISCUSSION POINT

When are some times your thoughts or emotions and your health seemed linked?

DISCUSSION POINT

What are some examples of being shaped by the culture? What messages do you want to shape your life? Explain.

WRITTEN REFLECTION

Have pens or pencils available. Provide paper for persons who do not have journals. Ask the group members to follow the instructions in the main text. Then ask them to share as much as feels comfortable with one other person in the group.

We Are What We Think

The Book of Philippians encourages us to think of things that are true, honorable, just, pure, pleasing, commendable, excellent, and worthy of praise. This counsel is not to be taken lightly. Our thought patterns affect our mental and physical health; we are what we think. A growing body of scientific evidence links thoughts and emotions to disease and health.

Long before the "positive thinking" movement existed and long before the establishment of Western medicine, Paul was encouraging Christians to think good and noble thoughts so that the God of peace would be manifested in their lives. He must have known that what we think about shapes our very being.

Today the choice is ours. We can choose to be shaped by God's Word or by the myriad of voices in our culture. One voice tells us we are valued no matter what we do or who we are; we are valuable simply because we are children of God. Another voice tells us we are valued only if we have certain physical characteristics, important jobs, large bank accounts, or fancy cars. Which message do you want shaping your life? If we choose to be shaped by God's Word, we know our life will be abundant no matter what our life's circumstance.

Written Reflection

What are the things that have shaped your life for better or for worse? In your journal or on a sheet of paper, write examples of how your thoughts or beliefs have shaped who you are.

Lectio Divina

Spiritual reading of God's Word is an excellent way to begin to let our lives be shaped and transformed into the life God intends for us. Known in Latin as *Lectio Divina*, spiritual reading is a practice with its roots in Judaism. In the sixth century Saint Benedict refined the practice and gave *Lectio Divina* a place of special importance in the Christian church. Literally, the term *Lectio Divina* means holy or sacred reading.

DISCUSSION POINT

What has been your experience with reading the Scriptures? Have you ever studied them in depth? Have you ever used the Scriptures for devotional reading?

The practice of *Lectio Divina* is the prayerful reading of the Holy Scriptures. This practice involves reading the Scriptures primarily as a devotional activity, not as a way of studying the Scriptures. *Lectio Divina* assumes that God is active in our life, interacting with each of us in order that we might be transformed into Christ's likeness. The premise of spiritual reading is that every passage of Scripture has the power to transform our daily experience because God is active in every piece of Scripture. Some of us have had a healing experience with Scripture at one time or another, but seldom in our regular reading have we experienced an encounter with the living God and almost never in certain passages. *Lectio Divina* provides us with a method for encountering the living God in every passage of Scripture.

This encounter with the living God through Scripture has direct implications for our daily life situation. Our bad habits are eliminated; we grow in our understanding of how God's Spirit works in our life; and we develop a greater capacity for compassion and love. However, these changes do not come quickly. It takes persistent practice of the spiritual discipline of *Lectio Divina* to experience these changes. Like persistent, gentle drops of water falling on hard rock, reading God's Word slowly transforms the hardness of our hearts. Gradually, we become more responsive to the steady stream of God's grace in our life and in the world.

Lectio Divina strengthens our relationship with God. This encounter with God forms the way we live in this world. If we stay with the discipline, we will gradually discover we are growing in our ability to have the mind of Christ as well as the heart of Christ. We are being shaped into the kind of human being God intends for us to be. *Lectio Divina* eventually transforms the way we view all of life, teaching us to experience God's grace in the ordinary.

WRITTEN REFLECTION

Instruct the group members to prayerfully consider the answers to the following questions before they write the answers. Inform them that these answers are for their eyes only; they will not share this information unless they choose to do so.

Which areas of your life would you like God to transform? Which areas of your life need the gentle, persistent presence of God's grace?

Listening for God

Lectio Divina involves listening to God's plan for your life through the Scriptures. This practice is a way of interacting with the Word of God as well as responding to what God offers you as daily nourishment. As you read, ask yourself, What is God's message for me? What is God trying to say to me through this text? With practice, you will begin to hear God speaking to you through the text.

DISCUSSION POINT

Has God ever spoken to you through the Scriptures? What was that experience like? In what ways have you experienced God talking to you?

How did God's message come to you at those other times?

Hearing God speak means you are beginning to discern God's message for your life. God's voice will come in many ways.

How might your experience with Lectio Divina *be different from other ways of listening to God? How might it be similar?*

How can you get away from reading in the way you usually read?

Sometimes you will find insight into how to be true to who you are in your particular circumstance; other times you will be given a clue to what the highest good is for a particular situation. When God speaks to you through *Lectio Divina*, what you receive is often so ordinary it seems anticlimactic. However, what you receive always enriches your life because you receive the presence of the living God.

As you begin to practice *Lectio Divina*, you may notice it is in direct opposition to your educational training. We have all been taught to read for information, to digest as much information from a text as possible in as little time as possible. In school we are taught to master a text, giving us full control over the content. In practicing *Lectio Divina*, we let the text master us. We are unconcerned with quantity of information; we want depth.

This kind of reading may seem unfamiliar and awkward to you. Instead of using your rational intellect to understand the text, you are to read from the heart and the spirit. While we are charged to love God with our mind, we are also instructed to love God with our heart and total being. In our culture we often place a priority on rational intellect at the cost of diminishing different ways of experiencing the world. Although studying the Bible and learning of its history can give our faith greater significance, in *Lectio Divina* we are more concerned with a heartfelt knowing than a rational understanding. I am not advocating an uninformed faith; I am making a plea to balance the rationality of our faith with the commitment of the heart.

Getting Started

Beginning to practice *Lectio Divina* requires an open heart, an open mind, and unhurried time. Your time is very personal, and it will be different for different people. This practice may feel comfortable, or it may feel laborious and unrewarding. As with any spiritual discipline, spiritual reading needs to be judged by its fruits. Does it produce in your life love, joy, peace, patience, kindness, generosity, faithfulness, gentleness, or self-control (Galatians 5:22)?

Selecting a Scripture passage is one of the first decisions you will need to make. Some persons prefer using a daily lectionary, because the passage is already selected and a lectionary can keep one from wasting the precious time set aside for devotions. Also a lectionary offers a wide variety of passages to meditate on over a period of time. If a lectionary is

GROUP INTERACTION

A lectionary is a list of Scripture readings for the church year. Have a lectionary available for the group members to see. Your minister may have a lectionary you could borrow for this session if you do not have one of your own.

What would be the advantages of using a lectionary? the disadvantages? What would be some advantages for you of choosing a particular book of the Bible? the disadvantages? Do you think you would prefer using a lectionary for this discipline or simply selecting one of the books of the Bible?

What time of day would be best for you? Where would be a good place for you to practice Lectio Divina? *What posture would be best for you? Which would detract from your experience?*

How will you manage to be unavailable to others so you can be available to God?

unappealing, perhaps you could start with the Psalms, Old Testament, Gospels, or Epistles. What is important is not jumping around. Choose your book or lectionary and stick to it. Remember, more than an accumulation of information, you are seeking transformation. Read only a small number of verses at a time—no more than ten or twelve. Be concerned with depth, not volume.

Time is needed in order to obtain depth. A minimum of thirty minutes is suggested; some persons find an hour works better. Whatever time you allot, God will put to good use if you give God your best. An hour when you are tired is not nearly as fulfilling as twenty minutes when you are fully awake. Choose a time of day in which you are most alert to practice this discipline. Also choose a posture that will facilitate a relaxed state of alertness. Sitting in a comfortable chair with your feet on the floor is a good way to begin.

Finding a place for solitude during your day may be the most difficult part of this spiritual discipline. With a multitude of demands on our time, finding a place and a time to be alone can become an arduous task. When you establish a time of solitude, do as much as you can to minimize the distractions. Give yourself permission to be unavailable to others so you can be fully present to God. Try unplugging the phone or letting the answering machine pick up messages. Barring any emergencies, ask your family to give you thirty minutes of undisturbed time; or have your secretary hold your calls. Turn off the television or radio and sink down into the silence. If silence is impossible to find, try using soft music to camouflage any surrounding noise.

Stop and release the activities of the day and the past few hours. Release yourself to God. Center in the silence. Instead of setting your own agenda for the time you have with this passage of Scripture, let God set the agenda. Be open to listening to God through the Scripture before you. Ask for God's guidance and for the illumination of the Holy Spirit.

Begin reading slowly. Sometimes reading aloud helps the mind to focus. Let word associations and images bubble up from your subconscious. Something significant may jump out at you. Let it happen; this is God's Word to you. If a thought continues to feel compelling, stay with it until it no longer feels pressing. Once you have the word or phrase, begin to digest it. Ask yourself, How does this apply to my life now? Why is this message important for me?

You may want to try imagining yourself in the biblical story. Which character are you? With whom do you identify? How do the characters feel about one another? What are the sights, sounds, and smells? What do you discover about yourself in the process?

From this encounter with Scripture and the living God, let a prayer emerge from your heart. Reflect on how this message moves you to pray for yourself and for others. When you have finished your prayer, release everything to God and simply sit in God's presence until it is time to resume your daily activities. As you leave the solitude, take the image, word, or phrase with you into your day. Let your reflection continue throughout the day; new insights may continue to emerge.

Practice and Written Reflection

Practice *Lectio Divina* by reading Romans 12:1-2. Afterward, record in your journal or on a sheet of paper any insights you receive.

Paul's Advice

In writing to the church at Rome, Paul gives some timeless advice. He wants the members of the church at Rome to present their bodies to God. To the Greek culture of Paul's day, this is a radical concept. The Greeks thought only the spirit mattered; at best the body was a prison to be tolerated. Paul writes that the body belongs to God just as much as the mind or spirit. He is implying that God wants the entire Christian—body, mind, and spirit—to be engaged in the act of worship.

Paul could be writing to us. Much like the Greeks, ours is a culture based on rational intellect. In a sense, Paul's plea to present our bodies for worship is a plea to us. When we practice *Lectio Divina*, we do exactly what Paul asked the church at Rome to do. We bring our whole selves to the worship and adoration of God. We listen to God with our heart as well as our mind.

The second verse of this passage speaks of the renewing of the mind. Paul believed that when a person became a Christian, his or her life had a new quality. The person had the mind of Christ; therefore that person was in the process of being transformed by Christ. Once a Christian, a person began to experience God's saving grace in new and exciting ways. The Christian was no longer bound by sin but freed by grace. The transformation of which Paul spoke is the same transformation that comes through the spiritual disciplines.

BIBLE STUDY

Ask the group if the instructions for Lectio Divina *are clear before beginning your practice.*

Participants will need their own Bibles so they can practice spiritual reading. Provide pens or pencils and paper. Suggest persons write in journals if they have them. Be sure to allow enough time to let participants experiment with this discipline. A minimum of ten minutes is needed; twenty minutes would be better. At the end of the allotted time, read the text aloud. Ask if any members of the group would like to share their experience or if anyone has any questions about the process.

After the group has shared, read the commentary provided on the passage. Does knowing something about the Greek culture of Paul's day affect your experience of Lectio Divina *with this passage? If so, how?*

Practice the Discipline

The only way to tell if spiritual reading is a discipline you will find helpful is to practice it on a regular basis. In the week ahead, set aside time each day to practice *Lectio Divina*. Make note, in the margin of this book or in your journal, of questions that arise as you experience this way of praying. When your partner for the week calls, share as much of your experience as you feel comfortable sharing. If, after talking to your partner, there are still things with which you need help, bring your concerns to the group next week.

Closing Worship

After a brief period of silence, ask group members to take turns reading a verse of Psalm 139:1-10 until the reading is completed.

CHAPTER TWO

PRAYER AND MEDITATION: THE FOUNDATION OF THE CHRISTIAN LIFE

WORSHIP

When the group is ready to begin, pray this prayer of Thomas Merton in unison.

CHECKING IN

Ask group members: What was your experience with Lectio Divina *over the past week? Did you have a chance to talk to your partner about your experience? Was it helpful to talk to someone?*

If anyone has any questions about the experience of Lectio Divina, take a few moments to address the questions as a group.

DISCUSSION POINT

Ask persons to read the section and to answer the following questions: Are you ready to be transformed by God? How do you think God might transform your life? What might you enjoy about a transformation? What might not be so good?

Prayer of Trust by Thomas Merton

My Lord God, I have no idea where I am going. I do not see the road ahead of me. I cannot know for certain where it will end. Nor do I really know myself, and the fact that I think that I am following your will does not mean that I am actually doing so. But I believe that the desire to please you does in fact please you. And I hope I have that desire in all that I am doing. I hope that I will never do anything apart from that desire. And I know that if I do this, you will lead me by the right road though I may know nothing about it. Therefore, will I trust you always, though I may seem to be lost and in the shadow of death. I will not fear, for you are ever with me, and you will never leave me to face my perils alone. Amen.

Are You Ready to Be Transformed?

The result of any spiritual discipline practiced over time is the transformation of the person. If you are one hundred percent happy with your life, do not undertake the disciplines of meditation and prayer because your life will change as a result. Both prayer and meditation help us become more aware of the unremitting movement of divine grace in our lives, and they enable us to be more responsive to the gentle, persistent presence of God. Prayer and meditation are major players in the transformation of human life.

▶

DISCUSSION POINT

What have you considered to be the purpose of prayer? How does your understanding of the purpose of prayer affect your prayer life?

Have you considered prayer as God's gift to you? If not, what difference might it make in your relationship with God if you would consider prayer a gift?

GROUP INTERACTION

Brainstorm various names for God with the group members. If you have a large piece of paper or a chalkboard, record the different names for God. See if the group can name a corresponding characteristic for each name.

Ask persons to evaluate silently their honesty with God. What feelings are they happy to share with God? What feelings and emotions do they prefer to hide? What has happened when they try to hide feelings from God? If anyone is willing, have those persons tell their thoughts and experiences.

Prayer: Communion With God

Prayer is the essence of the spiritual life, the fundamental activity for the Christian. Prayer is the vehicle for our relationship with God; we pray in order to be with God. Although we often ask God to fulfill our needs and desires, the primary purpose of prayer is not to receive that for which we ask. The primary purpose of prayer is to be with God.

As in a relationship between two people, our relationship with God grows best when we regularly set aside time to be with God. The more we communicate with the Divine and the Divine communicates with us, the more intimate our relationship will be.

Prayer is God's gift to us; God has given us prayer as a means of relating to the Source of divine love. Even our desire to pray is a gift of God, the result of God's Spirit working in our life moving us to commune with God.

Prayer and the Nature of God

How we pray depends on who we understand God to be. If we believe God is a merciless tyrant, we will hesitate to bring our frailties and failings to God's attention. We will not want to spend much time in God's presence at all. However, if we believe God is loving and full of mercy, we will approach God even when we have really made a mess of things. Our images of God affect the way we pray. It is important to make conscious our understandings of the Divine by listening to and examining our feelings when we pray or when we resist praying.

Jesus taught us to be as little children before God—open, trusting, and addressing God with unreserved honesty. Children have no difficulty expressing anger, doubt, or frustration. Some adults have learned to hide these emotions; we even try to hide these feelings from God. This is a foolish attempt. God knows our every thought and feeling. God wants us to be honest in our prayers. As we look at the Psalms, we see plenty of honesty. The psalmists wrote some of the most deeply intimate passages in the Bible. If we have trouble sharing some of our more difficult emotions and thoughts with God, reading the Psalms can help us overcome that difficulty.

When we pray, Jesus invites us to place ourselves in God's presence exactly as we are, warts and all. God will love us, and in the process our warts may be changed into beauty marks. The depth of God's mercy and inexhaustible love makes it possible for us to be forthright in God's presence. The more honest we are, the more intimate our relationship with God will be and the more we will know how much we are loved.

Prayer is immensely personal. Because everyone is different and because God reveals God's Self to us according to our needs, the structure and method of prayer will be different for different people. There are many kinds of prayer and many methods for praying. Breath prayer, centering prayer, intercessory prayer, silent prayer, prayer for guidance, contemplative prayer, and prayers of petition are but a few. When exploring the discipline of prayer, it is important to experiment until you find a prayer type that suits you. Let the Holy Spirit be your guide as you explore the discipline of prayer.

Bible Study

BIBLE STUDY

Ask the group members to read silently the passage from Luke, then ask someone to read it aloud. In pairs discuss answers to the following questions.

What lessons about God do you think Jesus intended for his disciples to learn from the Lord's Prayer? What does the Lord's Prayer teach you about God?

Read Luke 11:1-4.

In Jesus' day it was customary for a rabbi to teach his disciples a short prayer that they might habitually use. When Jesus taught the Lord's Prayer, he taught his disciples about the intimate and loving nature of God. He addressed God as "Abba" or "Daddy." The word *Father* fails to convey the full intimacy of the relationship that Jesus expressed in the original language.

Learning to Pray

There are effective and ineffective ways to pray. If we are open to God, the Holy Spirit will teach us to pray so our prayers will be useful. We will be guided to the right books, the right teachers. We will obtain insights about how to make our prayers effective.

The people in the Bible prayed as if their prayers made a difference. Praying was always in the positive, as if the condition already had been healed or the change already had occurred. Sometimes the prayers that resulted in healing in the Bible were more like direct commands. To the paralytic, Jesus said, "Stand up." To the man with the withered hand, Jesus said,

DISCUSSION POINT

Has God ever answered your prayers? For what did you pray? How did you experience the prayer being answered?

DISCUSSION POINT

Read 1 Corinthians 3:5-9 aloud. Ask the group members if this image of being a fellow-worker with God is a new understanding for them. If we are fellow-workers with God, does this affect our prayer life? How should we pray as God's fellow-workers?

DISCUSSION POINT

When was a time you prayed for a situation but failed to act? When was a time you acted but failed to pray? What happened? How do prayer and action go together to make both more effective?

Can you name a time when you had to wait for God to answer your prayer? How long did you have to wait? Are you still waiting?

"Stretch out your hand." People of the Bible prayed for others with the expectation that change would occur. When Jesus prayed for others he never prayed, "If it be thy will, . . ." He claimed the healing goodness of God already working in the lives of those whom he healed. When we use "if it be thy will," we are saying, "If this prayer doesn't work, we can blame it on God." We should use "if it be thy will" when seeking to discern God's will for a particular situation or when we are trying to get our wants out of the way of God's desires.

If we have not attuned ourselves to the Source of divine love before we pray, our prayers are pointless. We need to plug into the Source. If we do not commune with the Divine, our prayers are much like trying to send E-mail without a modem; the message goes nowhere. We need to learn how to be in contact with God, in relationship to God, so we can be a channel of divine healing love for ourselves and others.

The apostle Paul says we are "God's fellow-workers" (1 Corinthians 3:9, *The New English Bible*), implying that it is our responsibility to shape the world and to determine the outcome of events with God. Prayer is a powerful tool in helping God shape the world. Intercessory prayer, or praying for others, is the social dimension of prayer. It is an act of love for others that stretches us beyond ourselves in service to another.

If we are going to pray for any part of God's creation, we must listen for guidance. Often we rush into prayer without knowing what to pray for. If we do not hear the will of God for others, how can we pray for them? As fellow-workers with God, it is our responsibility to take time to listen so that we can know how to pray for our local communities, for the world's communities, for our leaders, for our churches, for those whom we love, and for the marginalized of society whom Jesus called "the least of these."

Praying for someone or something does not mean we are excused from acting. When we pray for a situation or a person, we also are responsible for doing all we can to bring about that for which we pray. It may take time for God's will to be manifested in the lives of those for whom we pray. We may be called to pray again and again, to persevere in our praying until God's will is realized in a particular situation. Sometimes blocks to God's grace must be removed before God's will can be manifested and our prayers answered. Waiting for God to remove the blocks to grace requires patience and persistence.

GROUP INTERACTION

Before beginning this section, ask the group members how they listen for God's voice in their lives. See how many different ways of listening you can name. If you have a large piece of paper or a chalkboard, make a list of them.

In the past, have you allowed time in your prayers to listen to God? Why or why not?

Ask one or more persons to tell about a time they listened to God through Scripture.

Ask one or more volunteers to tell about a time they listened to God through nature.

Ask one or more group members to tell about a time they listened to God through another person.

Have some persons tell about a time they heard God's voice through a thought that would not go away.

Ask persons who have heard God's message through a dream to tell about their experience.

Listening and Prayer

Often we talk too much in our prayers and do not take time to listen for God's response. Prayer is a conversation with God. As in any quality conversation, listening as well as talking is required.

Most of us have not been taught that listening is an essential part of prayer. Congregations have not stressed the listening side of prayer. In our corporate worship the time allowed for talking to God far outweighs the time we spend listening to God. Silence is all but absent in most worship services. Soren Kierkegaard wrote, "A man prayed, and at first he thought that prayer was talking. But he became more and more quiet until in the end he realized that prayer is listening."[1] Prayer requires our full attentiveness and willingness to listen to God.

There are many ways to listen to God. Scripture provides us with one of the more common ways of hearing God's word. We know when we have been addressed by God through Scripture when we are touched emotionally or helped in some way by what we have read.

Nature is another way to experience God's voice. When seeing God's creation in all its beauty, we can sense God's loving presence, reminding us we are not alone.

God also speaks to us through others. When the right person comes along at the right time, with the right phrase to help us out of a difficult situation or to move us into greater freedom and grace, we know God is speaking to us.

We also can hear God's voice through an intuition that will not go away. Often when someone comes into our thoughts repeatedly, it is God's way of nudging us to contact him or her, either for our benefit or theirs.

Dreams are another important way God speaks to us. Many biblical characters heard God's voice in their dreams. The same is true today as God often speaks to us through the images and symbols in our dreams. Our task is to interpret these symbols. Keeping a journal of our dreams can be of enormous help in understanding God's messages to us. The key to listening for God's voice is discernment, learning which voice is God's voice. With time and practice, we can become better at discerning the voice of God.

GROUP INTERACTION

Find out if anyone in the group has experienced any form of meditation. Ask if those persons will share their experiences. Then ask the group members to talk about the ways they listen to God.

Meditation: Be Still and Know God

Meditation teaches us to listen for God's voice in all that we do. In our hectic, fast-paced lives meditation can teach us to calm down and listen to God, regardless of what is happening around us.

When we feel overwhelmed by the demands on our time, slowing down and quieting down are things for which our spirits yearn. Stepping out of the crowd and finding stillness and silence is the only way for us to develop our relationship with God. As Jesus took time apart from the crowd to pray and meditate, we too are called to take time out of our pressing schedules in order to commune with God.

Even though we need solitude to meditate, meditation is not an escape from the world. Rather, it is the opportunity to contact the Source of all life so that we have the energy and guidance to live life fully. When we meditate, we create a space in our hearts for Christ to dwell. Often what we receive in meditation is so mundane and ordinary that it is far from an ecstatic experience. We might be encouraged to call someone who is difficult to contact, or we might be instructed on what to say to one of the children. Or we might receive a new awareness of God's love for us. Whatever the insight, meditation provides us greater perspective on our life in the world.

Simply stated, Christian meditation is listening to God and obeying God's will. Meditation involves being attentive to God who is speaking and who wants to address us; it is our way of hearing God's word. We need to be better listeners. Even when we find the time and place for solitude, it is difficult to silence the inner chatter long enough for God to get a word in. Christian meditation trains the mind to be silent and receptive to God; it teaches us to be good listeners.

Meditation is simple and uncomplicated; that does not mean it is easy. Focusing one's mind in a time of distractions is difficult. It takes concentration to participate in the mental activity of meditation. Christian meditation differs from meditation practiced by Eastern religions in a very significant way. In Eastern meditation, one is trying to empty the mind in order to find the center of one's being; in Christian meditation one attempts to fill the mind and heart with the Spirit of God. Christian meditation is a mental activity that leads us to prayer, to communion with God.

The simplest way to understand Christian meditation is to practice it. Sit in a chair with your feet on the floor in a relaxed but alert position. Place your hands comfortably in your lap.

GROUP INTERACTION

After the group understands the instructions for meditating, lead the group through a practice session. Keep the meditation time under five minutes; three minutes will probably be sufficient. When the group has finished meditating, have each person describe his or her experience. Did meditating feel natural to anyone? Was it a difficult experience? Is it something they would like to do again?

BEFORE NEXT TIME

Help each member of the group select a partner with whom to be in touch during the week ahead. Give the partners time to exchange names and phone numbers and to decide on a time when they can contact each other. Suggest they contact their partner at least once during the week to see how the experience of meditation and intercessory prayer is going.

WORSHIP

Close this session with prayer. Light a candle. Include thirty seconds of silence followed by intercessions from the group for the church, the world, and their families.

You might want to turn your palms upward to signify your willingness to receive what God wants to give to you. Close your eyes and breathe in deeply. As you inhale, imagine the love of God filling your entire being. As you exhale, let go of any tensions in your body and any stray thoughts. Silently, inwardly, begin to repeat, "Be still and know God." Listen to the words as you say them. If other thoughts or images distract you, gently return to the phrase, "Be still and know God." Use the phrase until you are sufficiently quieted or until you are aware of resting in God's presence.

As you begin to meditate, do not attempt to meditate for long periods of time. Three to five minutes is a long time for intense concentration when one is just beginning. Eventually, you can increase your time in meditation. You may also want to experience repeating different phrases from Scripture. Here are some suggestions:

"Peace! Be Still!"
"God leads me beside still waters."
"In quietness and confidence shall be your strength."
"Holy Spirit, fill me."
"Come, Lord Jesus."

Single words also work well for this kind of meditation. *Love, peace, joy, tranquility, compassion,* and *hope* are among my favorites. Experiment and see what feels right for you.

A growing relationship with the God of love can make a difference in transforming and freeing our lives from the burdens that cause us sleepless nights and worry-filled days. Transformation can happen in our world and in our life as we deepen our love relationship with God through prayer and meditation. Christ will come dwell in our heart and make all things new.

Before Next Week

In the week ahead set aside time each day to practice meditation and to pray for the members of your group.

[1]From *Soul Feast: An Invitation to the Christian Spiritual Life,* by Marjorie J. Thompson (Westminster John Knox Press, 1995); page 33.

CHAPTER THREE

FASTING: CREATING HOLY SPACE IN A LAND OF ABUNDANCE

WORSHIP

When the group is ready to begin, read this quotation and follow it with a minute of silence for personal prayer.

The Jewish Talmud says that after a person eats and drinks, he has but one heart, for himself alone. Before a person eats and drinks (when he is fasting) he has two hearts, one for himself and one for all the hungry people.[1]

CHECKING IN

Begin by welcoming any new persons to the group. If questions about prayer or meditation arise, see if the group's collective experience can address the issues at hand. If there are difficult questions, suggest that the person or persons make an appointment with the pastor.

Checking In

What was your experience with meditation? Did you and your partner have an opportunity to talk about your experiences? Was it helpful to have a partner? What else is happening in your life that you want the group to know?

WRITTEN REFLECTION

Before the group members begin reading about fasting as a spiritual discipline, ask them what they think about the discipline. Instruct them to record their answers.

Written Reflection

In your journal or on paper, record your initial impressions and feelings about fasting.

Hunger: The First Lesson About God

When my nephew was in his first year of life, he would wail with great discomfort between spoonfuls of food, so enormous was his hunger at mealtimes. No matter how hard one tried, the food did not get to his mouth or his stomach fast enough. Without even realizing it, my nephew learned his first theological lesson before he turned one year old. Hunger teaches us we are in a precarious position; we are dependent on something beyond ourselves for survival. Without food we cannot survive. Hunger informs us we cannot live without the help of God's creation; ultimately, we cannot live without reliance on God.

When we fast, we deprive ourselves of food. This discipline reminds us how deeply dependent we are on God. Without the help of God and God's creation, we will die. Fasting helps us put our relationships in order with God and all creation; it assists us in knowing where we fit into God's plan. Abstaining from food for spiritual purposes reminds us of the Source of our daily bread and puts things in perspective. Fasting helps us see where we choose to place our trust—in the material world or in the Creator of that world.

Less Is More

One trip down the bread aisle in the local supermarket makes "give us this day our daily bread" a multiple-choice decision. Advertisements on television keep images of food before our eyes. The diet industry has made a fortune from individuals who have consumed an abundance of calories. The food restaurants and supermarkets throw away could feed the hungry poor of this nation. We have a profusion of food in our culture. In a land of such excess, fasting seems like a foreign, if not antiquated, concept.

Why then should we fast? Fasting carves out a space in our life so there is room for God and God's gifts. If our life is too full, we cannot receive that which God has to give us. In this land of abundance our culture would have us believe we can have it all, do it all, and be it all. In a popular television commercial, three men say, "Done that; been there; tried that," implying they have conquered their limitations and have been everywhere and done everything under the sun. The commercial reflects the message of abundance. That message pushes us beyond our limitations and has many individuals working longer hours to acquire more and more material wealth. While looking for more, our spiritual life and personal relationships suffer from neglect. With the message of abundance being preached in our culture, the idea of willingly accepting limitations is not a popular one.

Fortunately, some members of our society are waking up to the lie that we must conquer all so we can have it all, do it all, be it all. In *Soul Feast*, Marjorie Thompson helps us see that some personal limits are life-restoring. Refusing to accept

DISCUSSION POINT

How does the concept of being totally dependent on God strike you? In what ways are we dependent on God?

DISCUSSION POINT

Name some of the excesses of our culture other than food. Which excesses may be crowding out your relationship with God?

DISCUSSION POINT

How can listening to our limitations promote life?

Can you name any life-restoring limitations?

What are some limits that you need to recognize in order to develop a fuller life?

these life-restoring limits can lead to emptiness, illness, and even death. Thompson states we cannot know the sovereignty of God if we cannot recognize our own limitations.[2] Fasting helps us recognize those limits that open us to life. We know it is necessary to set limits for children so they can grow into normal, productive members of society. Why, then, do we assume that as adults we no longer need to accept limitations? Accepting life-giving limitations increases our ability to live rich and abundant lives. The discipline of fasting helps us better understand those limitations.

The Judeo-Christian Tradition and Fasting

In ancient Jewish tradition fasting was used as penitence and as a way to repent of one's sin. At the time of the fall of Jerusalem, fasting helped remind the people why Israel had fallen and led them back into obedience to God. Individuals fasted, as did entire nations. Mosaic law directed that fasting was to be an integral part of the celebration of the Day of Atonement (Leviticus 23:27). Fasting enabled each person to encounter the will of God for his or her individual life.

When the people of Nineveh repented of their sin after hearing Jonah's preaching, they practiced fasting as a part of their repentance, hoping God would act mercifully. Fasting was a way to humble oneself before God and to invite God's favor at a time of crisis.

Fasting also was a way to prepare for challenges and important tasks. When Queen Esther prepared to petition the king on behalf of her people, she called a fast: "Go, gather all the Jews to be found in Susa, and hold a fast on my behalf, and neither eat nor drink for three days, night or day. I and my maids will also fast as you do. After that I will go to the king, though it is against the law; and if I perish, I perish" (Esther 4:16). The fast commanded by Queen Esther drew the community close to one another; it helped the Jews in Susa focus on the serious nature of their situation. Fasting helped Queen Esther gain strength for the job she had to do. She prepared herself inwardly, aligning her spirit and will with God's grace.

When Jesus was in the wilderness before beginning his ministry, he prepared to become a vehicle of God's grace for all God's creation through fasting and prayer. In Jesus' day fasting was a customary expression of the Jewish faith. In the Gospel of Luke the parable of the Pharisee and the tax collector recounts that the self-righteous Pharisee fasted twice a week. As the early church was born, Christian believers and leaders made frequent use of the discipline in private and corporate settings. After Paul met Jesus on the road to Damascus, Paul fasted and prayed for three days. Later, as converts were won to the faith and Christian communities began, Paul and Barnabas ordained leaders in the new churches by fasting and praying (Acts 14:23).

Jesus and the members of the early Christian church combined prayer with fasting, with notable results. The effectiveness of prayer seems to be greatly enhanced by the practice of fasting. Combining the two disciplines prepares us to live life at a deeper, more meaningful level.

As the Christian church grew, Easter became the central feast day. Christians prepared to celebrate by fasting. They were not to eat unusual foods, not even bread or oil. Only gruel and water were eaten from Good Friday until Easter, the day when catechumens were baptized and welcomed into the faith. The season of Lent grew out of this period of fasting.

Eventually, disputes arose over how many days Christians should observe a fast and what one should be allowed to eat. By the medieval period, the rules had become so strict and numerous that fasting became a hollow religious practice. More attention was paid to the proper diet and length of the fast than to the proper spirit of the fast. The creative, life-giving understanding of the fast practiced in the early church was lost in the legalism of the church.

The founders of the major Protestant traditions incorporated fasting into their religious practices. John Wesley is said to have fasted twice a week; tradition says that Martin Luther and John Calvin also fasted regularly. Some persons in the Roman Catholic tradition and Eastern Orthodox traditions still take fasting seriously.

DISCUSSION POINT

The modern church's understanding is that Lent is a period of prayer and self-denial. As Protestants, we sometimes are encouraged to give up things for the liturgical season, such as desserts, candy, television, or bad habits. In the early church the season of Lent was clearly a time of fasting and prayer. Is it possible that the feasting of Easter has lost its meaning because we have lost the fast? What would it mean to our celebration of Easter if Lent once again became a time of prayer and fasting?

BIBLE STUDY

Have persons read the Scripture passages and think about them. Before reading the commentary, ask the group members to record what they learned about fasting from reading the two passages of Scripture.

Bible Study

Read Matthew 6:16-18 and Luke 18:9-14.

Jesus taught his disciples about fasting; his teachings were clear and positive. The proper spirit for fasting does not include the pride of the Pharisee. The effort to gain public recognition of the Pharisee's fast was what Jesus strenuously opposed. The Pharisee's reward for his act of piety was his own pride, not his relationship with God. He considered himself righteous because of his actions, not God's grace. The Pharisee's fasting had become an external practice without the

GROUP INTERACTION

Ask members of the group if fasting is something they have ever tried or thought of trying. Invite them to share their feelings about fasting from food now that they know some of its history.

proper inward spirit. Jesus clearly required the outward act of fasting to match the inward attitude of humility; this was the proper spirit of fasting.

Before You Fast

Fasting along with prayer is a powerful way to open ourselves to the movement of God's Spirit in our life. It can empower us to do the will of God as it opens us to receive the grace of God. Fasting is a way of waiting on God. It expands our awareness of life and introduces us to life's deeper dimensions. The purpose of fasting is not to negate or denigrate the body; our bodies are gifts from God. The purpose of fasting is to make us sensitive to God's Spirit within and beyond our bodies.

Before beginning a fast, it is essential to have some basic information. Fasting is not harmful to the body if some common sense is used. Before fasting, check with your physician.

Do not attempt to fast if you are pregnant, ill, or have a weakened physical condition. Fasting lessens one's normal energies and should not be attempted when you need optimum energy to remain healthy. Normal activities may need to be curtailed to match your energy level while you fast. Stressful times in life are not good times to abstain from food.

Before you begin your fast, you may be tempted to load up on carbohydrates much like a marathon runner; that is a big mistake. It is better to eat light meals for a day or two before you fast. Also, abstaining from beverages containing caffeine for three days before you fast will eliminate a withdrawal headache at the time of the fast.

Fasting requires practice, as does any discipline. If you have never fasted, it is wise to begin with a twenty-four hour partial fast. A fast from lunch to lunch or dinner to dinner is a good way to start; only two meals are missed. Fresh fruit juices are excellent to drink during the fast, along with plenty of water. It is very important to drink a sufficient amount of water to keep your body hydrated and to flush from your body the toxins created when one fasts.

In the beginning you may be aware of how your body is responding to the fast; pay even closer attention to your attitudes. The attitude of the heart is most essential. While you fast, dedicate all you do during the day to the glory of God. Keep your heart focused on Christ. If it is possible, use the time normally given to meals and meal preparation to pray.

When it is time to break the fast, eat only a light meal of fresh fruits and vegetables, in small amounts at first.

After several weeks of partial fasting, you may want to try a normal fast of twenty-four hours, drinking only water. After having spiritual success with several normal fasts, you can do a thirty-six hour fast. In his book *Celebration of Discipline*, Richard Foster describes the dynamics of a longer fast and suggests it is best to discern through prayer if you are called to such a discipline.

Keeping track of your inner attitudes while fasting will help insure the fast you are keeping is motivated by the Spirit. Fasting as a means of God's grace brings into our life insights that deepen our relationship with and reliance on the Giver of all grace. Writing in a journal can be of enormous significance when we fast. It helps us focus on what is going on in our spirit as well as our body.

Abstaining from food makes us aware of how we use food for purposes other than keeping our body healthy. Some of us use food to repress uncomfortable feelings, to reward ourselves for a job well-done, to give us energy when we need sleep, or to subdue our restlessness. Fasting deepens our dependence on God when we are able to turn these insights over to God in prayer.

Fasting From Over Consumption

In *Addiction & Grace,* Gerald May uses the word *attachment* when speaking of addiction. He describes attachment as the displacement of spiritual longings onto things of this world. May says that addiction or attachment is a distorted spirituality. We recognize unhealthy attachments in our life as we become aware of those things or activities that control or consume us. When we try to fill our hungers with things of this world, we develop addictions.

Using material goods to fill our life and lessen our longings causes us to place greater priority on what is created than on the Creator. We loose sight of the One whose creation is called good, and God ceases to be the center and source of our life. When this happens, God's creation stops fulfilling its purpose of being a means of divine grace; creation becomes that which imprisons us.

Only God can fulfill our longings. We could benefit from the dynamic of fasting from those activities that are consuming

WRITTEN REFLECTION

Instruct the group members to list any areas of their life that are out of balance. Give them plenty of time to assess their life. Tell them to look for areas that they would like to change, even if the change is only minuscule. Do not hurry this exercise. Explain that the exercise is provided for their personal use. The more seriously they reflect on the question, the more helpful it will be.

GROUP INTERACTION

After the group members have finished taking stock of their life, instruct them to pair up with their partner for the week. Direct them to share with their new partner as much as they feel comfortable sharing. Suggest they contact their partner at least once during the week to see how the experience of fasting is going. Remind them to take a look at their hearts during their practice of fasting. Suggest that they might want to keep a journal of their experiences.

WORSHIP

Remember to light a candle as you move into worship. Explain there are many ways to worship, including singing. After a moment of silence, invite the group to sing a hymn.

us. Fasting from those things that devour us helps to bring our life back into balance. Abstinence from any substance or behavior creates room in our life for God; it restores a proper relationship between God's gifts and our use of them.

Fasting from those things that control us is not an attempt to deny enjoyment of God's gifts; it is a way to put God at the center of our life. Giving God recognition as the giver of all gifts leads us to greater freedom by releasing us from unhealthy attachments. Only by living a life centered in God will we experience the freedom and wholeness Christ offers.

Personal Reflection

List the excesses in your life. List those things that control you more than God does. Which of your activities are consuming you? Do you watch too much television? shop too often? work too much? exercise too much? drink too much? think about money or relationships too much? spend too much time on the computer?

Experience Fasting

There are many ways of fasting. Decide what kind of fast you want to experience during the next week. You may want to try the partial fast, or you may want to fast from one of the excesses in your life. Decide which will be most helpful to you. Remember, fasting teaches us that all our hungers are ultimately a hunger for relationship with God.

Closing Worship

Close this session by singing or reading the words to a hymn, such as "Hope of the World."

[1]From *The Jewish Kids Catalog*, by Chaya M. Burstein (The Jewish Publication Society of America, 1983); page 91.

[2]From *Soul Feast: An Invitation to the Christian Spiritual Life*, by Marjorie J. Thompson (Westminster John Knox Press, 1985); page 73.

CHAPTER FOUR

HOSPITALITY: AN EXPRESSION OF LOVE

WORSHIP

When the group is ready, form two sections. Have one section read the dark print and one section read the lighter print to use the adaptation of Saint Teresa's prayer as a responsive reading to begin this session.

CHECKING IN

Invite members of the group to share the highlights of their past week. After individuals have had time to discuss their personal experiences with the spiritual disciplines, ask what has happened in the past week that they want other group members to know about. What is coming up in their lives that they want to share with the group?

Christ has no body now on earth but ours;

Ours are the only hands with which he can do his work,

Ours are the only feet with which he can go about the world,

Ours are the only eyes through which his compassion can shine forth upon a troubled world.

Adapted from Teresa of Avila (1515–1582)[1]

Checking In

What was your experience with fasting? Did you keep a journal of your experience? Which spiritual discipline have you found the most helpful so far?

Hospitality in the Judeo-Christian Tradition

Though hospitality is not clearly defined in the Bible, it is referred to on many occasions. The rule of hospitality seems to have emerged from the life of the Hebrew nomads living in the desert. In order to survive, food had to be shared. Since there were few inns or "golden arches" in the desert, people depended on one another to provide the basic necessities of life. The rule of hospitality meant each person had a duty to provide food and shelter for the traveler even if the stranger at the door was your enemy. This desert code of ethics also meant one was bound to supply safe passage for your guest

What is your understanding of hospitality? Do you think the notion of hospitality is different today from what it was in the days of the Hebrew nomads? How is it different? How has it remained the same?

What do you think of the idea that Christianity might have stayed within Israel if persons had not provided hospitality to Jesus, Paul, and others?

Would you say that churches today are places that welcome different kinds of people and make them feel at home? Why or why not? How about our own church? How would you rate yourself on welcoming different kinds of people and making them feel at home in our church?

as long as he was on your land. It was a matter of survival—yours and the guest's.

In the ancient Near East, hospitality was offered to complete strangers. The dining table developed into a place of deep intimacy; eating with another meant you would never see that person as the enemy. Whenever you were at the table, there could be no enemies. If the stranger requesting hospitality at your door happened to be an enemy, he probably would have eaten alone. Even today, the most fundamental notion of hospitality is food; eating with others is often an act of friendship and love. When guests come into your home, it is customary to offer them food or drink.

The roots of hospitality extend into the history of our faith tradition. The very foundation of Christianity was built on hospitality. Jesus relied on the hospitality of others as he preached, taught, and healed. The apostle Paul depended on the generosity of others as he traveled about teaching and preaching the good news. Without the rule of hospitality, Christianity might have stayed within the confines of Israel.

In *Soul Feast*, Marjorie Thompson discusses how first century Christianity grew because of the power of the message of the gospel combined with the phenomenal caliber of Christian hospitality. The welcoming nature of new Christian communities provided a place for different kinds of people to feel at home and to be accepted in mutual love and support.[2]

Our Own Stories of Hospitality

As a teenager I moved with my family from a small town to a large city in the middle of a school year. I felt lost and alone in my new surroundings. With the school year already in progress, my classmates had made their friends for the year. Clubs were formed; groups were closed. It was a painful experience for me. The school administrator who ran the school supply store asked me if I would like to help her sell supplies to the students in the mornings before school. I gratefully said yes to the chance to have a place to belong in what I perceived to be a closed system. As I sold pencils and paper to students each morning, I met many new friends. Soon students recognized me as I walked through the halls and attended class; I was no longer the stranger in their midst. In her offer of a job the school administrator gave me the precious gift of hospitality. She gave me a place to be myself and a way to meet new friends in the middle of a school year already in progress.

GROUP INTERACTION

Form groups of two or three persons. Ask each individual to follow the instructions in the main text. Urge persons to be brief. Keep time, allowing each individual within the smaller groups no more than five minutes before moving to another person within their group.

Have representatives from the smaller groups share with the larger group insights gained about the nature of hospitality. Are there similarities among the groups in their experiences?

DISCUSSION POINT

Do you experience your community and/or neighborhood as hospitable or inhospitable? Explain.

What emotions do you experience when you are a stranger?

Can you recall a time when the mere act of listening to another initiated a friendship between you and someone else?

Think about three events in your life where hospitality was involved. Describe each event in a few sentences. Then answer the following questions:

1. <u>What are your experiences with providing hospitality? How did it make you feel to help someone else? Was the person to whom you offered hospitality a stranger? Did you provide the other person food? shelter? Did you receive anything in return for the hospitality you offered? Did the offer of hospitality change the nature of your relationship with the other person? How?</u>

2. <u>What are your experiences with receiving hospitality? When were you the stranger in need of hospitality? Did you know the person offering you hospitality? Was it difficult to receive kindness from another? What did it feel like to be on the receiving end of someone else's generosity? Did the experience change your relationship with the host?</u>

The Need for Hospitality

We live in a world of strangers. Our transient society has contributed to the breakdown of communities, making the person next door a stranger. Without the security of a community, persons look at others with suspicion. We have a real and pressing need for a hospitable place where individuals can live in community.

At one time or another, each of us has been the stranger. As children, when we first started school, we were the stranger in new surroundings, with new things to learn and new people to meet. In our society many of us have known what it is like to be the stranger when jobs call us and our families to new and unfamiliar places. As we age, we sometimes feel like strangers to ourselves, experiencing new emotions at different stages of life. Being the stranger is fundamental to the human experience.

One of the first tasks as we offer hospitality to others is to listen to their story, their bewilderment, their pain, and their joy. People are crying out to be heard and understood; they are estranged from themselves and from one another. Hospitality means listening with the goal of understanding the other as deeply as possible. In the act of listening with understanding, we are linked to one another. We find our common human needs overcome our differences. In the act of listening, strangers become friends.

DISCUSSION POINT

What is your definition of hospitality? How does your faith influence your understanding of hospitality?

The Essence of Hospitality

Henri Nouwen writes in *Reaching Out* that hospitality is "the creation of a free space where the stranger can enter and become a friend instead of an enemy."[3] Hospitality involves creating space in which others feel comfortable. Sometimes this means physical space. Often, it means emotional and spiritual space. Creating a safe place where others can feel at home to freely reveal their inner selves is the work of hospitality.

Hospitality is an expression of love. As we give hospitality, we offer the best of ourselves and our resources in openness and freedom. Hospitality does not force people to behave in specific ways or to believe certain things. Hospitality provides a space where the guests can grow into the persons God is calling them to be. To offer hospitality is to respect the other and the person's way of doing and being in the world. Hospitality allows the other to develop his or her own lifestyle; it does not force the guest to take on the lifestyle of the host. In the space of hospitality we meet the others where they are, not where we want them to be.

Hospitality involves caring for the whole person. Our concern for the body as well as the spirit helps others find their own path in life; hospitality can provide a place for others to heal from the emotional wounds of life. The classic elements of hospitality, as discussed in Thompson's *Soul Feast,* are food and drink, rest and shelter, protection and care, enjoyment and peace. These elements concern the whole person's well-being, not just the needs of the body.[4]

BIBLE STUDY

Form groups of three or four persons. Instruct the groups to read the texts from Matthew and Luke. Ask them to prepare answers to the questions in the main text. When the groups have had sufficient time to answer the questions, call them back together so they can share their findings.

The Bible and Hospitality

Jesus welcomed the strangers of his day with open arms. He spent his time with the lepers, the tax collectors, and the poor. Read Matthew 25:31-46 and Luke 10:25-37.

Biblical practices of hospitality had a particular concern with strangers, enemies, and the "least of these." How does our faith call us to treat the stranger? What is the consequence for us if we do not care for the stranger?

In a world where we view the stranger as a potential danger, it is difficult to offer hospitality. Aggression and violence have caused us to live in fear of those we do not know well. How do we maintain personal safety and still be obedient to the discipline of hospitality?

Who are the strangers in our midst today? Persons with AIDS? Gays and lesbians? The elderly? Those with different political views? with different native languages? different skin tones? The homeless? Those recently released from prison? Persons with different economic resources? Are persons of every class and size and color welcomed in your church? Who is the stranger in your congregation?

In a faith tradition that preaches the inclusive nature of God's love, it is precisely the welcoming of those who may be unwelcome in other settings that sets us apart. Scriptures make it clear we are to offer hospitality to all strangers, not just the ones who are dressed neatly and look like us. God sends us many strangers. How do we welcome these people?

The Gifts of Hospitality

Hospitality is a way of receiving God's presence. In Genesis 18:1-10, when the three strangers woke Abraham from his nap, Abraham brought them water to wash their feet. He asked Sarah to make them bread, and he sought a calf in the fields to roast. He then sat with the strangers as they ate. Though he had never met these people before, he treated them as honored guests. The three strangers Abraham and Sarah entertained at Mamre turned out to be three angels. They were messengers of God, revealing to Abraham and Sarah that God's promise would be fulfilled; Sarah was to give birth to a son. When we host the stranger, surprisingly we find we are not only bearers of God's word but receivers of it.

When we participate in the discipline of hospitality, we are in good company. Our mothers and fathers in the faith—all the way back to Abraham and Sarah—practiced the discipline of hospitality; therefore, we stand on holy ground and in a holy space. When we offer hospitality to the stranger, we often are surprised by the gifts the guest offers to us in the holy space of hospitality. Often we feel as if we have received more than we have given.

Biblical stories tell of authentic hospitality that welcomed the stranger into the home as an honored guest. They also report the wonderful gifts guests brought with them. For example, in 1 Kings 17:8-24, the widow of Zarephath gives food and shelter to the stranger Elijah. In return Elijah offers her an ample supply of oil and meal and raises her son from the dead. In Luke 24:13-35, the travelers on the road to Emmaus would not have known the blessing of the risen Christ if they had not

DISCUSSION POINT

Can you name a time when you offered hospitality to another and felt you received more than you gave?

BIBLE STUDY

Read these two Scripture passages aloud in the group: 1 Kings 17:8-24 and Luke 24:13-35. Discuss the following questions: Christ often comes to us in the stranger. Can you name a time this has happened to you? What gift did you receive?

offered hospitality to the stranger who joined them on the road. Because they welcomed the stranger into their home, they recognized Jesus as they shared in the breaking of the bread and received God's gift to them.

Hospitality means receiving as well as giving. The guest shares the gift of grace with the host, and in the mutual giving and receiving community is born.

Hospitality and Our Relationship With God

DISCUSSION POINT

In what ways are you too busy or preoccupied to receive God's gifts?

Receiving God's gifts is one way we can offer hospitality to God. This receiving is more difficult than meets the eye. When we become so preoccupied with our agenda, we remain unaware of what God is trying to give us; we are not free to receive God's gifts. If we are too busy, our life will not be a hospitable one; we need to create a hospitable space where we can receive God and God's gifts. Most of us are afraid of too much space in our life, so we fill our days with activity and noise. What we really fear is loneliness, and we mistake emptiness and space for loneliness. However, loneliness begins when there is no room in our busy schedules; we become strangers even to ourselves.

When we make ourselves available to the Divine and listen for God's word to us, we provide hospitality for the Creator of the universe. Once we have heard God's word, responding in loving obedience to what we have heard provides further hospitality for God.

The first gift of hospitality was God's creation of this wonderful world, filled abundantly with everything we need for our pleasure and nurture, and God's invitation to us to partake of these wonderful gifts. The natural response to this gift of hospitality is gratitude. The way we treat our neighbor, the stranger, our earth home, and all its inhabitants expresses our gratitude and love for God. We return God's hospitality when we offer hospitality to the stranger and to one another.

Hospitality Begins at Home

DISCUSSION POINT

How do you extend hospitality to family members?

What do you need to do to make your home more hospitable to all family members?

The need for hospitality in the home may be a new understanding of this discipline. Our children are not ours to own; they belong to God. For a brief time they are our most important guests. Within each of them is a seed of promise that needs nurture and patience so the child can unfold into the person he or she was created by God to be. It takes much time and love to make these "little strangers" feel at home.

Offering hospitality for the child means creating a space that is receptive to the child's needs and providing healthy boundaries within which the child can grow. As children are encouraged to trust their inner selves, they develop the tools that will enable them to leave home and to continue their journey as fellow travelers through life.

Hospitality for the World

Hospitality begins at home, but it does not end there. There are many ways and places in which we can provide hospitality for our world. Our churches are called to embody the hospitality God has shown us in Christ. Do visitors and strangers feel welcome in your congregation? Do members feel appreciated? Is your church inclusive of all members of society? What can you do to make your church a more hospitable place?

The work place also needs hospitality. Are creative ideas received well by those in charge? Do people listen openly to one another? Are individuals respected? Is the physical space comfortable? What can you do to practice the discipline of hospitality where you work?

In our neighborhoods there are many opportunities to offer the gift of hospitality. Last summer, three people on our street organized a neighborhood picnic. The result is that the neighborhood now feels more like a community. Neighbors look after one another. Friendships are being formed and favors are being exchanged. What can you do in your neighborhood to be hospitable?

There is a crying need for hospitality in this world. People need adequate food, shelter, and clean water. The number of homeless in the United States continues to grow. Refugees from wars continue to need a safe place of hospitality. Health care is not available to the poor. Education is not equally accessible to bright young minds. Making this world a more hospitable place is what Jesus calls us to do; it is a response to God's love for us. What can you do during the week to make God's creation a place of hospitality for the stranger?

[1]From *Eerdman's Book of Famous Prayers*, compiled by Veronica Zundel (William B. Eerdmans Publishing Company, 1983); page 51.

[2]From *Soul Feast: An Invitation to the Christian Spiritual Life*, by Marjorie J. Thompson (Westminster John Knox Press, 1995); page 121.

[3]From *Reaching Out: The Three Movements of the Spiritual Life*, by Henri J. M. Nouwen (Doubleday & Company, Inc., 1975); page 51.

[4]From *Soul Feast*; page 122.

GROUP INTERACTION

Invite the members to choose a partner for the week ahead, and give them time to exchange phone numbers. Instruct the members to select one aspect of the discipline of hospitality to practice during the week ahead. Have them share their selection with their partner. Invite the partners to check in on one another during the week to see how the practice of hospitality is going.

WORSHIP

Close this session by lighting a candle and by asking persons to offer prayers of intercession for the strangers of our world. Include one minute of silence.

CHAPTER 5

SPIRITUAL GUIDANCE: THE SEARCH FOR MEANING

WORSHIP

When the group is ready to begin, open the session by praying this prayer in unison. You may use a prayer of your own if you choose.

CHECKING IN

Invite the group members to share significant events that may have occurred in their life since the last meeting. Ask them to respond to the questions in the main text.

WRITTEN REFLECTION

Have you ever felt the need for a deeper experience of your faith? Write about that time now. What did you do to try to meet your need? What was happening in your life? If you are satisfied with the current expression of your faith journey, record the different components of your faith that nurture you.

Prayer for Discernment

Grant me, O Lord, to know what is worth knowing,
to love what is worth loving,
to praise what delights you most,
to value what is precious in your sight,
to hate what is offensive to you.
Do not let me judge by what I see,
nor pass sentence according to what I hear
but to judge rightly between things that differ,
and above all to search out
and do what pleases you,
through Jesus Christ our Lord. Amen.

Thomas à Kempis (1380?–1471)

Checking In

Anyone who has ever given a party or entertained guests knows hospitality is hard work. <u>Was your experience of practicing hospitality difficult? What did you do? How do you feel about the experience? As a discipline, is hospitality something you feel called to practice?</u>

The Need for Something More

There is a growing awareness in the church of the need for spiritual formation. People are hungry for meaning and purpose they have not been able to find in the ordinary ways. With a long history in the Judeo-Christian tradition, spiritual guidance may be the answer for those who seek a deeper experience of faith.

DISCUSSION POINT

Has anyone provided spiritual guidance for you in the past? Explain. Have you provided spiritual guidance to anyone? If so, tell about that experience.

The Christian Tradition and Spiritual Guidance

Traditionally, teachers and rabbis have provided spiritual guidance or spiritual direction for seekers of the faith. Jesus offered direction to his disciples, providing for us a model of spiritual guidance. Through intimate relationships, he helped the twelve disciples experience the presence of God in ways that changed their life. He was both friend and teacher, master and servant; Jesus shared his life with those he served and taught.

As the church grew, Paul provided spiritual guidance for new Christian communities. He nurtured new converts with spiritual milk and gave more mature believers the solid food of knowledge of the Spirit. Paul encouraged others to grow into the likeness of Christ, to increase in their knowledge and love of God.

In the fourth through the sixth centuries, people traveled in the wilderness for miles to seek advice from Christian hermits who sought the solitude of the wilderness to grow in greater likeness to Christ. Pilgrims sought guidance from these holy individuals to discern the will of God for their lives. Later in the church's history, monks, priests, and elders in the church practiced spiritual guidance. Today, both laity and clergy are called to the ministry of spiritual guidance.

GROUP INTERACTION

Brainstorm with members of the group the different ways they discern God's presence in their life. If you have a large piece of paper or a chalkboard, record their ideas.

When to Seek a Spiritual Director

In the life of faith we find many sources for discerning the presence of the living God in our life. Corporate worship, small covenant or prayer groups, private and public Bible studies, reading Christian books, personal prayer, and the indwelling presence of Christ are all ways we seek to experience and articulate the presence of God in our life.

At times, however, we may experience a need for something more. Like the pilgrims who sought guidance from Christian hermits, we may need to seek guidance from another who shares the Christian journey. Sometimes corporate worship and personal efforts to make sense of God's presence in our life do not seem to be enough to still the restlessness and fulfill the inner yearning. That may be the time to seek the help of a spiritual director. When our prayers do not seem to be working for us, or when we want to be more intentional about the spiritual life, a spiritual director can help.

What Is a Spiritual Director?

A spiritual director is someone who lives the life of the Spirit and understands some of its complexities—someone who can help us find direction and meaning. Spiritual directors serve as teachers, helping the directees learn to discern and articulate their own experience of God. A spiritual director is a person who has navigated the sea of faith and who can assist others in avoiding some of the pitfalls and temptations of the Christian life. Thomas Merton wrote that the first duty of the spiritual director is to look at his or her own inner life and to take time for prayer and meditation.[1] One cannot lead others successfully into areas where one has never been.

Spiritual directors nurture, challenge, pray for, and help their directees stay accountable to a disciplined life of faith. While their job is to listen and respond to the movements of faith in the life of the directee, spiritual directors realize that the Holy Spirit is the true spiritual director. During a session of spiritual guidance, both the director and the directee sit in the presence of the Spirit of God, waiting for God to be made known. Together, they wait to see where God is present in the life of the directee.

DISCUSSION POINT

Have you ever sought to know the will of God for your life with another person's support? What was that like? Do you think having a companion for your faith journey would be helpful?

Bible Study

BIBLE STUDY

Form small groups of three or four persons. Have each person read the Scriptures listed in the main text. Instruct the members to discuss in their small group the questions following each Scripture.

"For where two or three are gathered in my name, I am there among them" (Matthew 18:20). Jesus gave his disciples the assurance of his presence with these words. In spiritual direction, when two people gather to discern the presence of God, they meet with the assurance of Jesus' companionship and guidance. <u>What difference does it make to know that Christ is present when two or three gather in his name? How do you think acknowledging the presence of Christ affects a session of spiritual direction?</u>

"But speaking the truth in love, we must grow up in every way into him who is the head, into Christ . . ." (Ephesians 4:15). <u>What does it mean to grow up into the likeness of Christ? Do you have persons in your life who "speak the truth in love" and who help you mature in your faith? Who are they and how have they helped you?</u>

What Is Spiritual Direction?

Spiritual direction is not psychotherapy, neither is it pastoral counseling. In *Spiritual Friend*, Tilden Edwards includes a chart[2] developed by Dr. Gerald May to help understand the differences between therapy or counseling and spiritual direction. While there may be some overlapping concerns, there are many remarkable differences. Both therapy and counseling can be healing tools, in and of themselves; but they are not to be confused with spiritual direction. Spiritual direction always focuses on one's relationship with God. In the midst of the events and crises of life, God is always at the center of spiritual direction.

	Psychotherapy	Pastoral Counseling	Spiritual Direction
SUBJECT	Disordered patient wanting cure	Disordered (troubled) client wanting help	A soul searching for God; not a disorder but a sacred situation
GOAL	Resolution of psychic conflict and adjustment to society (Medical Model).	Healing, sustaining, reconciling, and guiding. (More holistic model).	Being and becoming in God.
METHOD	Techniques employed on client for desired results.	Helping acts resulting in benefit to client.	Allowing self and relationship to be a vehicle of grace, of the will of God. Primary method: surrender, letting go of whatever is in God's way.
ATTITUDE OF HELPER	Responsible for cure of patient. *My* will be done.	Client or the relationship is responsible. *Our* will be done.	Only God is responsible for whatever healing/growth occurs. *Thy* will be done.

GROUP INTERACTION

Have the group study the chart in the main text and then answer the question below the chart.

Using the chart as a guide, discuss the differences between spiritual formation and therapy or counseling. <u>Can you think of situations when a person might need to seek therapy or counseling rather than spiritual direction?</u>

Spiritual direction is a means of grace by which we learn the inward teachings of the Holy Spirit. Spiritual direction is rooted in hope—the hope that the road will rise to meet us as we take the next step on the journey of life. Spiritual direction is about letting go, releasing those things that bind us and taking hold of the only thing that can bring us freedom—Christ Jesus.

Our daily experiences are the raw material for spiritual direction. In a direction session we tell the stories of our life. We talk about those things that made us into who we are today—for good or ill; and we seek to discern God's presence in all the events of life. Because the nature of spiritual direction is so personal, it is important to feel safe and comfortable discussing the details of our life and God's presence in them. It is not always easy to talk about God. Our inner thoughts are sacred, and we need to feel we can trust our spiritual director with them. Confidentiality is central to the director-directee relationship.

WRITTEN REFLECTION

Ask persons to write in their journals or on paper a response to the following question. Give them adequate time to think before writing an answer. What would you say to a spiritual director if you had an opportunity to speak to one?

The First Step Is Prayer

If you have never been to a spiritual director, there are a few things to keep in mind. One begins to locate a spiritual director through prayer. If you are interested in spiritual direction, ask God if this is the right move for your life now. Articulate why you feel the need for a spiritual director. Are you responding to the promptings of God? Or is this one more thing to do on your self-improvement list? Once you find a spiritual director, you can assess your decision to begin spiritual direction in the first few sessions.

A Few Things to Think About

Selecting a spiritual director is a personal process similar to finding a good physician. You want someone who is experienced and trustworthy. The relationship has to feel right.

Seek a person who has a sense of maturity, one who is also on the spiritual journey. The person need not be an ordained minister. Many lay persons are well-suited to the ministry of spiritual direction. The person you select need not be employed as a spiritual director; however, it should be someone who embodies a life of faithfulness to the gospel.

Ask persons to write their thoughts in their journals or on paper. Their comments will not be shared with any- one unless they choose. Allow plenty of time for persons to think before answering the following questions:

Who do you know who could be a spiritual director for you? Using the information in the main text, list the qual- ities you want in a spiritual director. Do you want your spiritual director to be a man or a woman? Are you looking for a spiritual director who is older than you? the same age? younger?

Seek a good listener who can hear without being judgmental and who is not easily shocked at a wide range of human behaviors. God works in all kinds of ways. A good spiritual director knows how to see God, even in that which others name as suspect.

Spiritual direction is not about domination and submission. A person who is bossy, who demands his or her suggestions be followed, is not going to be a good spiritual director. Find someone who trusts that God is working in your life as well as his or hers and who knows that God's grace is abundant. Someone who trusts your ability to discern God's presence in your life will be of much help to you.

Honesty is important. When difficult things need to be said, when we need to be held accountable for our behaviors, a spiritual director who is not afraid to speak the truth is a valu- able companion. Sometimes it is not easy to hear when we have been less than accountable in our spiritual life, but it is necessary if we are going to grow into the likeness of Christ.

It will be helpful if you and your spiritual director form a covenant in your early sessions. The covenant should include the number of times you agree to meet before evaluating the relationship. Usually six times is an adequate number of ses- sions to discover if you are working well with your spiritual director.

The covenant could also include the frequency and length of your sessions. Some people like to meet every four to six weeks for sixty to ninety minutes. If distance makes it difficult to meet, less frequent sessions of greater length are possible. Decide what works best for you.

How does prayer function in your relationship? Do you know if your spiritual director is praying for you? Are you going to pray for your spiritual director and your time together? These decisions can be part of your covenant.

Some spiritual directors charge; others do not. Clarify this issue during the first session. Decide how to use your time together. Will prayer be a part of your time together? Will your director be for you a teacher? friend? comforter? parent? listener? Make your expectations known in the early sessions; these may be things to include in a covenant.

GROUP INTERACTION

Invite the members to choose a partner for the week ahead, and give them time to exchange phone numbers. Instruct the members to contact their partner sometime during the week in order to discuss the need for a spiritual director in their life. If they feel comfortable, they can share with each other what they might say to a spiritual director.

WORSHIP

If the group has grown more comfortable with silence, consider extending the silent prayer to two minutes or more.

Companions on the Journey

Christianity is not a solitary path; we need companions for the journey of faith. Jesus did not try to live a faithful life alone. He chose twelve friends with whom to share his life and faith. Sometimes we need the focused attention of one person to assist us during times of crisis or intentional growth. Other times, we find gatherings for worship and Bible study sufficient for our needs. No matter where we are in our faith, the journey is less tiresome and more joyful when we share it with one another.

Closing Worship

Light a candle. Include an extended period of silence, then close with the following prayer or one of your own.

A Prayer of Saint Patrick

Christ be with us, Christ be before us, Christ be behind us,
Christ in us, Christ beneath us, Christ above us,
Christ on our right, Christ on our left,
Christ where we lie, Christ where we sit, Christ where we arise,
Christ in the heart of every one who thinks of us,
Christ in every eye that sees us,
Christ in every ear that hears us.
Salvation is of the Lord,
Salvation is of the Christ,
May your salvation, O Lord, be ever with us. Amen.

Saint Patrick, Ireland 5th Century, ALT[3]

[1]From *Spiritual Friend,* by Tilden H. Edwards (Paulist Press, 1980); pages 128-29.

[2]From *Spiritual Friend,* page 130.

[3]From *The United Methodist Book of Worship,* 1992. Copyright © 1992 by The United Methodist Publishing House; #529. Used by permission.

CHAPTER SIX

WORSHIP: PRAISE AND THANKSGIVING

WORSHIP

When the group is ready to begin, open the session by singing the hymn printed; or you may use another hymn or a prayer of your own.

CHECKING IN

Pose to the group the questions in the main text and wait for responses. Try not to put anyone on the spot; let those who wish to answer do the talking.

DISCUSSION POINT

Ask the group members to define worship. List their responses on a large piece of paper or a chalkboard.

Sweet, Sweet Spirit

*There's a sweet, sweet Spirit in this place,
and I know that it's the Spirit of the Lord;
there are sweet expressions on each face,
and I know they feel the presence of the Lord.
Sweet Holy Spirit, sweet heavenly Dove,
stay right here with us, filling us with your love;
and for these blessings we lift our hearts in praise;
without a doubt we'll know that we have been revived
when we shall leave this place.[1] Amen.*

Checking In

<u>After thinking about spiritual direction for a week, how do you feel about the idea? Is it something you would like to pursue? Did you contact your partner this week? What did you talk about?</u>

Our Purpose in Life

We are created to worship and to praise God; this is our first priority in life. The word *liturgy*, which we use to describe the prayers and readings of a worship service, means the work of the people. Worship is our work; it is our job to give honor and glory to God.

Worship is our response to God's love. The word *Eucharist*, which we use to refer to the portion of the liturgy called the Lord's Supper, means "thanksgiving." Gratitude is a natural response to any gift, including the gift of God's love in Jesus Christ. When we realize the enormity of the gifts God has offered to us, we naturally respond in praise and thanksgiving. As we experience gratitude to God in every cell of our body, we understand what worship is and the work of the people becomes almost effortless.

Although we often equate liturgy with rituals, rituals or the lack of them do not make worship a reality. Worship is a matter of the heart; it is God's Spirit stirring within our hearts. Even the best liturgy cannot make worship happen until the Spirit of God moves within us. Singing, praying, and preaching may facilitate worship; but these things do not become worship until God's Spirit touches ours. Even as we respond to the divine love, we are dependent on God's initiative in order to worship.

BIBLE STUDY

Select someone to read the text aloud.

Form groups of three or four persons and discuss the following questions:

How does the understanding of "the heart" from the ancient Jewish tradition affect the way you interpret Jesus' commandment? If worship is a matter of the heart, how does this understanding affect the way you view worship? Is worship in our church a matter of the heart? Do you agree or disagree that we are dependent on God even for our ability to worship?

Bible Study

Read Mark 12:28-30.

In *Soul Feast*, Thompson writes that in ancient Jewish tradition an individual's heart was understood to be the center of the personality. Thought, desire, motive, feeling, and even a person's will were perceived to originate from the heart.[2] A heartfelt thanks meant responding with one's whole being. When Jesus commands us to love the Lord with all our heart, soul, mind, and strength, it is a commandment encompassing every molecule of our being. No part of us should hold back from loving God.

Often worship in our churches does not appeal to the whole person; it focuses on the intellect. God calls us to worship with our whole being, to feel free to laugh and to cry in worship, to express our emotions. Sometimes we may need to kneel, bow in reverence to the cross, or extend our palms upward to express awe and wonder toward our Creator God. Other times we may want to clap with joy after a moving musical presentation. God gave us bodies as well as minds to use in worship; we need to feel free to do so.

Worship as a Discipline

When we worship, we express our love for God and we obey Jesus' commandment. We put God first in our life. True worship can take place in any setting; it can be part of our daily routine. If we live with the attitude of loving God in all we do, everything we do becomes an act of worship. However, it takes time and practice to develop this perspective. This is what makes worship a discipline; we have to develop a worshipful outlook on life through disciplined practice.

WRITTEN REFLECTION

Ask persons to think about the following questions and to write answers in their journals or on paper. How do you practice gratitude in your life? Are there set times to offer thanksgiving to God? What about spontaneous thanksgivings? How would practicing gratitude change your life?

The more we rehearse an activity, the more quickly it becomes second nature to us. If worship is a matter of the heart, developing times during the day to offer gratitude to God will increase the room for God's presence in our life. The more we acknowledge God's grace in our life, the more room there is for God's grace. Our awareness of God's presence increases as our gratitude increases. Our feelings often follow our actions. Even when we do not feel particularly thankful, once we express gratitude, our hearts open to God's love. Practicing gratitude is an excellent way to begin to exercise the discipline of worship.

First Things First

The times the community gathers to praise God become occasions to affirm the importance of community in the Christian faith. We are, after all, the body of Christ; and the body is made of many parts. Christians do not live in isolation. Jesus lived in the midst of community and calls us to do the same. When we gather for worship, God's Spirit breaks through our isolation and joins us together in the priesthood of all believers. We become one in the Spirit.

As we gather in worship to remember the saving acts of God in Jesus Christ, many of us come wanting inspiration to get us through the week. We come seeking, hoping, and praying for something to sustain us in the days ahead. Often, we come with little or no preparation for the hour we spend in worship. Some of us have not prayed or listened to God all week long. We want to be filled with God's love and Spirit during the hour we set aside to worship God. Sometimes we are disappointed. We leave the worship service feeling as empty as when we arrived. If the gathered community worship is the only time during the week when we pay attention to our spiritual life, it is no wonder we leave empty-handed. We have our priorities out of order.

In *Celebration of Discipline*, Richard Foster writes of the "holy expectancy" the people of the Bible experienced when they gathered together for worship.[3] The community gathered knowing they would meet and experience the presence and power of God. They seldom were disappointed because they experienced the power and presence of God during the entire week. They lived with a "holy expectancy." In all their daily activities they experienced the presence of God—why should worship be any different?

In modern times we have our priorities skewed. We live most of our moments with little awareness of God's presence or power. Intellectually, we might know God is working in our lives. We might even have faith in the God of the Old and New Testaments, but often we do not experience the reality of God's love—especially during the times we gather for worship. In order for gathered worship to be meaningful and inspirational, we must prepare prior to the service. We must cultivate a "holy expectancy" in all we do during the week. If we experience God's presence in our life when we are working, eating, sleeping, or relaxing, we will experience God's presence when we worship too.

Preparing for Worship

If worship is the work of the people, we have our job cut out for us. While we may have little power over the form of worship in our congregation, we certainly can contribute to the spirit of worship. Here are a few suggestions of what you can do to prepare for the Sunday service:

1. Pray for your pastor and worship leaders and for the gathered community. Daily prayers can dramatically change the experience of worship for the entire congregation, not just the person praying. Invoking God's Spirit in the planning of worship has a cumulative effect. The more we acknowledge and seek God's Spirit in the planning of worship, the more likely we are to experience God's presence at the actual time of worship.

2. If you know the Scripture for the coming Sunday, use it as a devotional reading during the week. Meditate on the Scripture and study it. Even reading the Scripture before hearing it on Sunday morning can increase its meaning in our life. If you do not know the Scripture before the Sunday service, start praying the Scriptures. Use *Lectio Divina* as the practice of your personal devotion. Your familiarity with Scripture will enhance your experience of corporate worship.

3. If you know the hymns before the service, incorporate them into your devotional life. Try praying the hymns of the church; read the lyrics as if they are prayers.

4. Listen for God's voice during the week. Try to discern where God is moving in your life. Practice cultivating an awareness of God's presence as you go about your daily routine. Imagine Jesus is sitting next to you in your car as

you do your errands or drive to work. Carry a cross in your pocket to remind you of Christ's abiding presence. Silently offer sentence prayers as you work, or silently pray for those with whom you come in contact during the day. Look for the Spirit of Christ in the eyes of those you meet. There are many ways to cultivate an awareness of God's presence. Find a way that works for you.

5. Arrive at church several minutes before worship is to begin. Use the time to focus on God and to center yourself for worship. Pray for what is about to happen and for those who will lead the gathered community in worship. As the sanctuary fills with members of the gathered community, pray for those who enter. Surround them with the light of Christ.

These activities can increase our awareness of God's presence in our common worship. Worship is not an isolated part of our Christian life; it is one important aspect of it. Learning to be open to God's presence during the week will enhance our experience of worship on Sunday morning.

The Fruits of Worship

Worship changes us. It places us in the presence of God, and that is always a life-changing experience. The changes may be gradual or dramatic, but we always are changed into the likeness of Christ Jesus as we worship God.

When we worship, God calls us into obedient servanthood. Worship is meant to return us to the world so we might be servants of justice and mercy, ambassadors for Christ. Like seeds, we are scattered to grow and produce the fruit of Christ's love in the world. If our worship does not move us to be the church in the world, then it has missed the mark. If we do not become more obedient to God's yearnings for our life, we have not fully worshiped.

Sabbath Time

Read Exodus 20:8-10a.

Honoring the sabbath may be one of the most frequently broken of the Ten Commandments. We try to pack more into a day than time allows. We work overtime. We squeeze an extra hour out of the day by robbing ourselves of needed sleep. We

DISCUSSION POINT

Which of the suggestions for preparing for worship sound interesting? Which could you incorporate into your life?

DISCUSSION POINT

Does our church's worship enable us to be the church in the world? How do you represent Christ for others?

BIBLE STUDY

Read the passage from Exodus aloud. Before you continue reading, ask the group to define sabbath time.

WRITTEN REFLECTION

After the group has studied this section, have persons write answers to the following questions in their journals or on paper. After persons have finished, ask them to turn to the person next to them and to share as many of their answers as they choose.

How do you use time? Do you feel as if you have enough time to accomplish what needs to be done? Do you feel time is your friend or your enemy?

What does it mean to you to "honor the sabbath and keep it holy"?

How do you think sabbath time and leisure time differ? How do you spend your leisure time? How does the way you spend your leisure time differ from the way you spend sabbath time?

DISCUSSION POINT

Do you view worship as entertainment? Explain.

sometimes try to do more than one thing at a time. We take work home with us or continue to work on our vacations. We use Sunday as a day to accomplish chores we did not have time to do during the other six days of the week.

Time is treated as a commodity in our society, as something to be bought and sold. Those who have wealth can buy leisure time by paying for services like lawn care and housecleaning. Those who are poor spend much of their time trying to survive; leisure is not an option for many of the poor. However, we are not commanded to honor leisure time; we are commanded to honor sabbath time. While both sabbath and leisure can include resting from our normal activities, the motivation for the two is different. Leisure time implies that we are the master of it; sabbath time belongs to God.

Honoring the sabbath means setting time aside to acknowledge and worship our Creator God. Sabbath time is holy time. Sabbath time is accessible to both the rich and the poor. Honoring the sabbath is a way of life. Claiming time to honor God helps us to put life in perspective by acknowledging that God is the giver of all good things. We realize our place in God's grand plan when we honor the sabbath. We then are able to cease our frenetic activity and to live life abundantly. When we honor the sabbath, we place our trust in God to provide for our needs.

The sabbath is intended both for our benefit and for God's benefit. As we are renewed by sabbath rest, we are freed to fully worship our Creator. God longs for us to honor the sabbath because God yearns for us to worship God.

Worship and Entertainment

We live in an entertainment culture. Television and the cinema condition us to expect to sit back, relax, and be entertained in all areas of life. When worship does not entertain us, we feel worship is dry and boring. Worship is not meant to be entertainment; we are to take part in worship as active participants, not as passive viewers.

Television provides us with an interesting dilemma. Church worship services broadcast across the airwaves provide a wonderful service for those who are unable to join the gathered community for worship. Shut-ins and the ill can participate in worship from their homes and hospitals. However, the broadcasting of worship services can reinforce the erroneous belief that worship is entertainment. We cannot let the electronic church be a substitute for the body of Christ. We need to find ways to include in the life of the church those who are ill or otherwise unable to join the gathered community on Sunday mornings.

Although worship is not entertainment, it can be an enjoyable experience if we are willing to put some effort into it. After all, worship is our most important work as Christians.

Concluding the Study

GROUP INTERACTION

Form groups of three or four persons and discuss the questions in the main text.

This study has ended, but our spiritual journey continues. <u>What have you learned in this study that will help you continue to grow in your faith? Which spiritual discipline will you be most likely to incorporate into your life?</u>

How will you continue to find support for your spiritual life? Discuss a plan of action that will help you get the support you need. You might consider covenanting with one or two others to meet on a weekly or monthly basis. You might want to seek the help of a spiritual director. <u>Are there other options available to you?</u>

Closing Worship

WORSHIP

Close this session by lighting a candle. Invite the participants to stand or sit in a circle and to join hands. Include several seconds of silence, then invite each person to offer a prayer. If participants choose not to pray verbally, instruct them to squeeze the hand of the person next to them, signaling to the next person their turn to pray. When individuals have finished offering their personal prayers, invite everyone to pray the Lord's Prayer in unison.

[1]From *The United Methodist Hymnal*. Copyright © 1989 by The United Methodist Publishing House; #334. Used by permission.

[2]From *Soul Feast: An Invitation to the Christian Spiritual Life*, by Marjorie J. Thompson (Westminster John Knox Press, 1995); page 54-55.

[3]From *Celebration of Discipline: The Path to Spiritual Growth* (revised edition), by Richard J. Foster (Harper & Row, 1988); page 161.

THE LIFESEARCH GROUP EXPERIENCE

Every LIFESEARCH group will be different. Because your group is made up of unique individuals, your group's experience will also be unique. No other LIFESEARCH group will duplicate the dynamics, feelings, and adventures your group will encounter.

And yet as we planned LIFESEARCH, we had a certain vision in mind about what we hoped might happen as people came together to use a LIFESEARCH book for discussion and support around a common concern. Each LIFESEARCH book focuses on some life concern of adults within a Christian context over a six-session course. LIFESEARCH books have been designed to be easy to lead, to encourage group nurture, and to be biblically based and needs-oriented.

Each chapter in this LIFESEARCH book has been designed for use during a one and one-half hour group session. In each LIFESEARCH book, you will find
• times for group members to "check in" with each other concerning what has gone on in their lives during the past week and what they wish to share from the past week concerning the material covered in the group sessions;
• times for group members to "check in" about how they are doing as a group;
• substantial information/reflection/discussion segments, often utilizing methods such as case studies and simulation;
• Bible study segments;
• segments in which a specific skill or process is introduced, tried out, and/or suggested for use during the week to come;
• segments that help group participants practice supporting one another with the concerns being explored.

LIFESEARCH was not planned with the usual one hour Sunday school class in mind. If you intend to use LIFESEARCH with a Sunday school class, you will need to adapt it to the length of time you have available. Either plan to take more than one week to discuss each chapter or be less ambitious with what you aim to accomplish in a session's time.

LIFESEARCH was also not planned to be used in a therapy group, a sensitivity group, or an encounter group.

> A LIFESEARCH group is simply a group of persons who come together to struggle together from a Christian perspective with a common life concern.

No one is expected to be an expert on the topic. No one is expected to offer psychological insights into what is going on. However, we do hope that LIFESEARCH group members will offer one another support and Christian love.

We will count LIFESEARCH as successful if you find your way to thought-provoking discussions centered around information, insights, and helps providing aid for living everyday life as Christians.

You might find it helpful to see what we envisioned a sample LIFESEARCH group might experience. Keep in mind, however, that your experience might be quite different. Leave room for your creativity and uniqueness. Remain receptive to God's Spirit.

You sit in the living room of a friend from church for the second session of your LIFESEARCH group. Besides you and your host, four other persons are present, sitting on the sofa and overstuffed chairs. You, your host, your group leader, and one other are church members, although not all of you make it to church that regularly. The remaining two persons are neighbors of the leader. You chat while a light refreshment and beverage are served by the host.

Your leader offers a brief prayer and then asks each of you to share what has been going on in your lives during the past week since you last met. One member shares about a spouse who had outpatient surgery. Several mention how hectic the week was with the usual work- and family-related demands. Prayer concerns and requests are noted.

This session begins with a written reflection. The leader draws your attention to a brief question in the beginning of the chapter you were assigned to read for today. Group members are asked to think about the question and to write a short response.

While the leader records responses on a small chalkboard brought for that purpose, members take turns sharing something from their written reflections. A brief discussion follows when one group member mentions something she had never noticed before.

Group members respond as the leader asks for any reports concerning trying out the new life skill learned in the previous session. Chuckles, words of encouragement, and suggestions for developing the new skill further pepper the reports.

The leader notes one of the statements made in the assigned chapter from the LIFESEARCH book and asks to what extent the statement is true to the experience of the group members. Not much discussion happens on this point, since everyone agrees the statement is true. But one of the members presses on to the next statement in the LIFESEARCH book, and all sorts of conversation erupts! All six group members have their hot buttons pushed.

Your leader calls the group to move on to Bible study time. You read over the text and then participate in a dramatic reading in which everyone has a part. During the discussion that follows the reading, you share some insights that strike you for the first time because you identify with the person whose role you read.

You and the other group members take turns simulating a simple technique suggested in the book for dealing with a specific concern. Everyone coaches everyone else; and what could have been an anxiety-producing experience had you remained so self-conscious, quickly becomes both fun and helpful. You and one of the other group members agree to phone each other during the week to find out how you are doing with practicing this technique in real life.

It's a few minutes later than the agreed upon time to end, but no one seems to mind. You read together a prayer printed at the end of this week's chapter.

On the way out to your car, you ponder how quickly the evening has passed. You feel good about what you've learned and about deepening some new friendships. You look forward to the next time your LIFESEARCH group meets.

This has been only one model of how a LIFESEARCH group session might turn out. Yours will be different. But as you give it a chance, you will learn some things and you will deepen some friendships. That's what you started LIFESEARCH for anyway, isn't it?

STARTING A
LifeSearch GROUP

The key ingredient to starting a LifeSearch group is *interest*. People are more likely to get excited about those things in which they are interested. People are more likely to join a group to study and to work on those areas of their lives in which they are interested.

Interest often comes when there is some itch to be scratched in a person's life, some anxiety to be soothed, or some pain to be healed.

Are persons interested in the topic of a LifeSearch book? Or, perhaps more important to ask, do they have needs in their lives that can be addressed using a LifeSearch book?

If you already have an existing group that finds interesting one of the topics covered by the LifeSearch books, go for it! Just keep in mind that LifeSearch is intended more as a small-group resource than as a class study textbook.

If you want to start a new group around LifeSearch, you can begin in one of two ways:

- You can begin with a group of interested people and let them choose from among the topics LifeSearch offers; or

- You can begin with one of the LifeSearch topics and locate people who are interested in forming a group around that topic.

What is the right size for a LifeSearch group? Well, how many persons do you have who are interested?

Actually, LifeSearch is intended as a *small-group* resource. The best size is between four and eight persons. Under four persons will make it difficult to carry out some of the group interactions. Over eight and not everyone will have a good opportunity to participate. The larger the group means the less time each person has to share.

If you have more than eight persons interested in your LifeSearch group, why not start two groups?

Or if you have a group larger than eight that just does not want to split up, then be sure to divide into smaller groups of no more than eight for discussion times. LifeSearch needs the kind of interaction and discussion that only happens in small groups.

How do you find out who is interested in LifeSearch? One good way is for you to sit down with a sheet of paper and to list the names of persons whom you think might be interested. Even better would be for you to get one or two other people to brainstorm names with you. Then start asking. Call people on the telephone. Or

> **Interest often comes when there is some itch to be scratched in a person's life, some anxiety to be soothed, or some pain to be healed.**

visit them in person. People respond more readily to personal invitations.

When you invite persons and they seem interested in LIFESEARCH, ask them if they will commit to attending all six sessions. Emergencies do arise, of course. However, the group's life is enhanced if all members participate in all sessions.

LIFESEARCH is as much a group experience as it is a time for personal learning.

As you plan to begin a LIFESEARCH group, you will need to answer these questions:

- **Who will lead the group?** Will you be the leader for all sessions? Do you plan to rotate leadership among the group members? Do you need to recruit an individual to serve as group leader?

- **Where will you meet?** You don't have to meet at a church. In fact, if you are wanting to involve a number of persons not related to your church, a neutral site might be more appropriate. Why not hold your meetings at a home? But if you

do, make sure plans are made to hold distractions and interruptions to a minimum. Send the children elsewhere and put the answering machine on. Keep any refreshments simple.

- **How will you get the LIFESEARCH books to group members before the first session?** You will want to encourage members to read the first chapter in advance of the first session. Do you need to have an initial gathering some days before the first discussion session in order to hand out books and to take care of other housekeeping matters? Do you need to mail or otherwise transport the books to group members?

Most LIFESEARCH groups will last only long enough to work through the one LIFESEARCH book in which there is interest. Be open, however, to the possibility of either continuing your LIFESEARCH group as a support group around the life issue you studied or as a group to study another topic in the LIFESEARCH series.

TIPS FOR LIVELY DISCUSSIONS

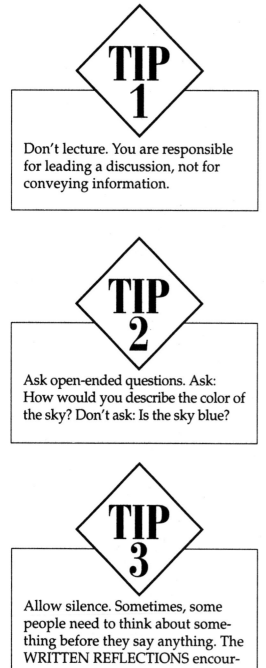

TIP 1

Don't lecture. You are responsible for leading a discussion, not for conveying information.

TIP 2

Ask open-ended questions. Ask: How would you describe the color of the sky? Don't ask: Is the sky blue?

TIP 3

Allow silence. Sometimes, some people need to think about something before they say anything. The WRITTEN REFLECTIONS encourage this kind of thought.

TIP 4

Recognize when the silence has gone on long enough. Some questions do fall flat. Some questions exhaust themselves. Some silence means that people really have nothing more to say. You'll come to recognize different types of silences with experience.

TIP 5

If Plan A doesn't work to stimulate lively discussion, move on to Plan B. Each chapter in this LIFESEARCH book contains more discussion starters and group interaction ideas than you can use in an hour and a half. If something doesn't work, move on and try something else.

TIP 6

Let the group lead you in leading discussion. Let the group set the agenda. If you lead the group in the direction you want to go, you might discover that no one is following you. You are leading to serve the group, not to serve yourself.

Ask follow-up questions. If some-one makes a statement or offers a response, ask: Why do you say that? Better yet, ask a different group member: What do you think of so-and-so's statement?

Do your own homework. Read the assigned chapter. Plan out possible directions for the group session to go based on the leader's helps in the text. Plan options in case your first plan doesn't work out. Know the chapter's material.

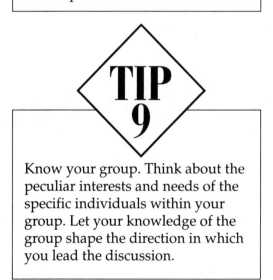

Know your group. Think about the peculiar interests and needs of the specific individuals within your group. Let your knowledge of the group shape the direction in which you lead the discussion.

Don't try to accomplish everything. Each chapter in this LifeSearch book offers more leader's helps in the form of DISCUSSION POINTS, GROUP INTERACTIONS, and other items than you can use in one session. So don't try to use them all! People become frustrated with group discussions that try to cover too much ground.

Don't let any one person dominate the discussion—including yourself. (See "Dealing With Group Prob-lems," page 58.")

Encourage, but don't force, persons who hold back from participation. (See "Dealing With Group Prob-lems," page 58.)

TAKING YOUR GROUP'S TEMPERATURE

How do you tell if your LIFESEARCH group is healthy? If it were one human being, you could take its temperature with a thermometer and discover whether body temperature seemed to be within a normal range. Taking the temperature of a group is more complex and less precise. But you can try some things to get a sense of how healthily your group is progressing.

✓ **Find out whether the group is measuring up to what the members expected of it.** During the CHECKING IN portion of the first session, you are asked to record what members say as they share why they came to this LIFESEARCH group. At a later time you can bring out that sheet and ask how well the LIFESEARCH experience measures up to satisfying why people came in the first place.

✓ **Ask how members perceive the group dynamics.** Say: On a scale from one as the lowest to ten as the highest, where would you rate the overall participation by members of this group? On the same scale where would you rate this LIFESEARCH group as meeting your needs? On the same scale where would you rate the "togetherness" of this LIFESEARCH group?

You can make up other appropriate questions to help you get a sense of the temperature of the group.

✓ **Ask group members to fill out an evaluation sheet on the LIFESEARCH experience.** Keep the evaluation form simple.

One of the simplest forms leaves plenty of blank space for responding to three requests: (1) Name the three things you would want to do more of. (2) Name the three things you would want to do less of. (3) Name the three things you would keep about the same.

✓ **Debrief a LIFESEARCH session with one of the other participants.** Arrange ahead of time for a group member to stay a few minutes after a meeting or to meet with you the next day. Ask for direct feedback about what seemed to work or not work, who seems to be participating well, who seems to be dealing with something particularly troubling, and so forth.

✓ **Give group members permission to say when they sense something is not working.** As the group leader, you do not hold responsibility for the life of the group. The group's life belongs to *all* the members of the group. Encourage group members to take responsibility for what takes place within the group session.

✓ **Expect and accept that, at times, discussion starters will fall flat, group interaction will seem stilted, group members will be grumpy**. All groups have bad days. Moreover all groups go through their own life cycles. Although six sessions may not be enough time for your LIFESEARCH group to gel completely, you may find that after two or three sessions, one session will come when nothing seems to go right. That is normal. In fact, studies show that only those groups that first show a little conflict ever begin to move into deeper levels of relationship.

✔ **Sit back and observe.** In the middle of a DISCUSSION POINT or GROUP INTER-ACTION, sit back and try to look at the group as a whole. Does it look healthy to you? Is one person dominating? Does someone else seem to be withdrawn? How would you describe what you observe going on within the group at that time?

✔ **Take the temperature of the group—really!** No, not with a thermometer. But try asking the group to take its own temperature. Would it be normal? below normal? feverish? What adjective would you use to describe the group's temperature?

✔ **Keep a temperature record.** At least keep some notes from session to session on how you think the health of the group looks to you. Then after later sessions, you can look back on your notes from earlier sessions and see how your group has changed.

LifeSearch Group Temperature Record

Chapter 1
_____
_____
_____

Chapter 4
_____
_____
_____

Chapter 2
_____
_____
_____

Chapter 5
_____
_____
_____

Chapter 3
_____
_____
_____

Chapter 6
_____
_____
_____

DEALING WITH GROUP PROBLEMS

What do you do if your group just does not seem to be working out?

First, figure out what is going on. The ideas in "Taking Your Group's Temperature" (pages 56-57) will help you to do this. If you make the effort to observe and listen to your group, you should be able to anticipate and head off many potential problems.

Second, remember that the average LIFESEARCH group will only be together for six weeks—the average time needed to study one LIFESEARCH book. Most new groups will not have the chance to gel much in such a short period of time. Do not expect the kind of group development and nurture you might look for in a group that has lived and shared together for years.

Third, keep in mind that even though you are a leader, the main responsibility for how the group develops belongs to the group itself. You do the best you can to create a hospitable setting for your group's interactions. You do your homework to keep the discussion and interactions flowing. But ultimately, every member of the group individually and corporately bears responsibility for whatever happens within the life of the group.

However, if these specific problems do show up, try these suggestions:

✓ One Member Dominates the Group
• Help the group to identify this problem for itself by asking group members to state on a scale from one as the lowest to ten as the highest where they would rank overall participation within the group.

• Ask each member to respond briefly to a DISCUSSION POINT in a round robin fashion. It may be helpful to ask the member who dominates to respond toward the end of the round robin.

• Practice gate-keeping by saying, "We've heard from Joe; now what does someone else think?"

• If the problem becomes particularly troublesome, speak gently outside of a group session with the member who dominates.

✓ One Member Is Reluctant to Participate
• Ask each member to respond briefly to a DISCUSSION POINT in a round robin fashion.

• Practice gate-keeping for reluctant participants by saying, "Sam, what would you say about this?"

• Increase participation by dividing the larger group into smaller groups of two or three persons.

✓ The Group Chases Rabbits Instead of Staying With the Topic
• Judge whether the rabbit is really a legitimate or significant concern for the group to be discussing. By straying from your agenda, is the group setting an agenda more valid for their needs?

- Restate the original topic or question.

- Ask why the group seems to want to avoid a particular topic or question.

- If one individual keeps causing the group to stray inappropriately from the topic, speak with him or her outside of a session.

✔ Someone Drops Out of the Group

- A person might drop out of the group because his or her needs are not being met within the group. You will never know this unless you ask that person directly.

- Contact a person immediately following the first absence. Otherwise they are unlikely to return.

✔ The Group or Some of Its Members Remain on a Superficial Level of Discussion

- In a six-session study, you cannot necessarily expect enough trust to develop for a group to move deeper than a superficial level.

- Never press an individual member of a LifeSearch group to disclose anything more than he or she is comfortable doing in the group.

- Encourage an atmosphere of confidentiality within the group. Whatever is said within the group stays within the group.

✔ Someone Shares a Big, Dangerous, or Bizarre Problem

- LifeSearch groups are not therapy groups. You should not take on the responsibility of "fixing" someone else's problem.

- Encourage a member who shares a major problem to seek professional help.

- If necessary, remind the group about the need for confidentiality.

- If someone shares something that endangers either someone else or himself/herself, contact your pastor or a professional caregiver (psychologist, social worker, physician, attorney) for advice.

IF YOU'RE <u>NOT</u> LEADING THE GROUP

Be sure to read this
article if you are *not*
the person with
specific responsibility
for leading your
LIFESEARCH group.

If you want to get the most out of your
LIFESEARCH group and this LIFESEARCH
book, try the following suggestions.

✓**Make a commitment to attend all the
group sessions and participate fully.** An
important part of the LIFESEARCH experience takes place within your group. If you
miss a session, you miss out on the group
life. Also, your group will miss what you
would have added.

✓**Read the assigned chapter in your
LIFESEARCH book ahead of time.** If you
are familiar with what the MAIN TEXT of
the LIFESEARCH book says, you will be able
to participate more fully in discussions and
group interactions.

✓**Try the activities suggested in
BEFORE NEXT TIME.** Contributions you
make to the group discussion based upon
your experiences will enrich the whole
group. Moreover, LIFESEARCH will only
make a real difference in your life if you
try out new skills and behaviors outside of
the group sessions.

✓**Keep confidences shared within the
group.** Whatever anyone says within the
group needs to stay within the group. Help
make your group a safe place for persons
to share their deeper thoughts, feelings,
and needs.

✓**Don't be a "problem" participant.** Certain behaviors will tend to cause difficul-
ties within the life of any group. Read the
article on "Dealing With Group Problems,"
on pages 58-59. Do any of these problem
situations describe you? Take responsibility for your own group behavior, and
change your behavior as necessary for the
sake of the health of the whole group.

✓**Take your turn as a group leader, if
necessary.** Some LIFESEARCH groups will
rotate group leadership among their members. If this is so for your LIFESEARCH
group, accept your turn gladly. Read the
other leadership articles in the back of this
LIFESEARCH book. Relax, do your best, and
have fun leading your group.

✓**Realize that all group members exercise leadership within a group.** The health
of your group's life belongs to all the
group members, not just to the leader
alone. What can you do to help your group
become healthier and more helpful to its
members? Be a "gatekeeper" for persons
you notice are not talking much. Share a
thought or a feeling if the discussion is
slow to start. Back off from sharing your
perspective if you sense you are dominating the discussion.

✓ **Take responsibility for yourself.** Share concerns, reflections, and opinions related to the topic at hand as appropriate. But keep in mind that the group does not exist to "fix" your problems. Neither can you "fix" anyone else's problems, though from time to time it may be appropriate to share insights on what someone else is facing based on your own experience and wisdom. Instead of saying, "What you need to do is . . ." try saying, "When I have faced a similar situation, I have found it helpful to . . ."

✓ **Own your own statements.** Instead of saying, "Everyone knows such and so is true," try saying "I believe such and so is true, because . . . ." Or instead of saying "That will never work," try saying, "I find it hard to see how that will work. Can anyone help me see how it might work?" Instead of saying, "That's dumb!" try saying, "I have a hard time accepting that statement because . . . ."

DOING LifeSearch
IN ONE HOUR OR LESS

If you have already read "The LIFE-SEARCH Group Experience" on pages 49-51, you will have discovered that LIFESEARCH is designed for use in sessions of at least one and one-half hours in length. Or, if you have already tried to lead a LIFESEARCH session in a Sunday school class, you may have felt frustrated at so much material to cover in so little time. What do you do if you want to use LIFESEARCH in a Sunday school class or other setting that offers one hour or less?

You can choose from among three basic options:

—OPTION 1: Divide each session into two or more shorter sessions,

—OPTION 2: Abbreviate each session, or

—OPTION 3: Save LIFESEARCH for a longer time period than Sunday school allows.

✔ Dividing Sessions

If you want to cover all the material in the LIFESEARCH book but you do not have the luxury of one and one-half hour or longer sessions, you may want to divide each session as it appears in the book into shorter sessions. The downside is that your class or group will need more than six weeks to complete the study. Classes on a quarter structure might want to consider this option, however, and plan for twelve to thirteen weeks studying one LIFESEARCH book.

Once you choose to divide sessions, you will then have to decide at what point you are going to break off each session. Again, you have a couple of good possibilities:

—Break off wherever you happen to be at quitting time. Mark that place in your book, and resume there the following week.

—Assign approximate times to each learning option found in the marginal notes. If you have only forty-five minutes for your session, find and mark the point in your book where you will need to stop after roughly forty-five minutes of class time.

You will probably want to keep in some time at the beginning of each session for "checking in" as well as some time at the end for worship and prayer.

✔ Abbreviating Sessions

ThThe option of abbreviating sessions will work best if you are limited to six sessions of one hour or less. Your dilemma will be to decide what material and learning options you will cover and what you will leave out.

Look at the learning options found in the marginal notes as items in a learning menu. Consider the goals of your group in choosing this LIFESEARCH book to study, the amount of time you have in your session, the interests of the individuals in your group, and the ways in which those individuals learn best. Not everyone learns best by means of reading and discussion! Some persons prefer to learn with more active and interactive learning methods. On the basis of these considerations, choose those learning options from the margin that will work best with your particular group within the time limitations you have.

The greatest danger leaders in this situation face is that they will be tempted to choose only those learning options they like or with which they feel comfortable. For the sake of the other members in your group, try stretching yourself and select learning options that will best fit *their* needs.

✔ Saving LIFESEARCH for Another Occasion

The curriculum planners who put together the LIFESEARCH approach believe that LIFESEARCH works best in time segments of at least one and one-half hours. This amount of time permits groups to develop *as groups.*

The content of your LIFESEARCH book is only part of what makes up your study experience. Yes, we hope that you will learn new knowledge and discover new skills to put into practice. But we also hope you will find nurture and support among the unique individuals who make up your group. The dynamics of your small community are important to your growth as a human being and as a Christian disciple.

Ideally, we would like to see your group continue meeting and helping one another beyond the time when you run out of materials from the six chapters of this book. You might want to try another LIFESEARCH study. Or, you might want simply to meet together weekly, biweekly, or monthly to talk about personal issues, struggles, and moments of growth concerning your LIFESEARCH topic.

Keep in mind that saving LIFESEARCH for a setting outside of Sunday morning and when you have more time than one hour may be what you and your group need to do. The choice of how you use LIFESEARCH belongs to you and your group.

OUR LifeSearch GROUP

Name	Address	Phone Number